LAND OF THE FREE

By

Lynn Santer

First published in 2003 by Zeus Publications Australia
http://www.zeus-publications.com
P.O. Box 2554, Burleigh MDC Qld. 4220
Australia

This is a work of fiction based on a true story.
Any resemblance to any persons living or dead is not entirely coincidental.

Lynn Santer (left) with **Tippi Hedren** (star of Alfred Hitchcock's "The Birds" turned big cat conservationist) and **Meryl Harrison** (right)

Chapter 1

Charlene Tynsworth mopped her brow, noticing the familiar shimmer in the air. It was as though she was inside nature's cooking pot. The heat was unbearable, but for Charlene the weather was the least of her problems. The donkey she was tending to had been badly gashed by a barbwire harness, an injury the likes of which she had seen a hundred times before. The donkey hardly flinched; it was as if she knew the gentle carer was trying to help her.

Although Charlene wanted to berate the farmer who owned the donkey for his heartlessness, instead she remained calm. Charlene understood economic realism was the only rationale a native Zimbabwean struggling to put food on the table would understand. At least he hadn't sold the beast to be used as bait for hunters who would have tied her to a tree, left to be nibbled alive for days before the prey animal stepped into their trap. Too many donkeys had unfortunately suffered that gruesome fate.

For a fleeting moment she thought back to her privileged life in Los Angeles. It seemed impossible that in this day and age anyone could be struggling to put food on the table, impossible to think that ten thousand miles away the biggest problem was making sure one was only seen in the latest designer fashions, and impossible beyond comprehension to accept that most of her former friends didn't even want to know about the horror faced by both man and beast and this far off land.

None of Charlene's friends had approved of this American beauty leaving her affluent lifestyle to devote herself to the conservation of endangered animals. Only one person kept in touch with her: Hollywood legend of the sixties, Joan Taylor. Joan too had given up many of her privileges to devote herself to the conservation of endangered animals. However, unlike Charlene, Joan remained in the US, preferring to try and change the legislation that allowed irresponsible private ownership of these magnificent creatures, which often led to the animal being discarded like garbage.

Joan had created a sanctuary for these cast-offs, where she currently cared for over sixty big cats and one elephant that had gone mad in a circus. But aside from Joan, it seemed no one wanted to hear about Charlene's quest to help stop the rapid march to extinction of many of God's magnificent creatures. Their attitude seemed to be: why complicate a life already so full of deadlines and back-biting with issues that after all only affect mere animals in a country many would never even visit?

Over time, Charlene had become more and more isolated, gradually losing all faith in humanity. She'd lived in the harsh climate and even harsher environment of Zimbabwe for ten years, engaging in her back-breaking, soul-destroying, thankless labor of love. Yet despite this, her face retained a youthful glow. There was nothing tanned, leathery or harsh about her appearance. Her soft brown eyes showed no bitterness, no despair. She'd cropped her lush auburn hair short, so that now it framed her kind, gentle face like a radiant aura.

Her one true friend, her dog Shaka, whimpered. The little Jack Russell terrier could sense Charlene's anguish and shared her pain.

"Don't worry, Shaka, she'll be okay," she said kindly.

While the native farmer looked on from under the shade of an ancient tree, Charlene examined the extent of the injuries. She mopped her brow again, gently removed the barbwire harness from the bleeding donkey and tended to its wounds.

"I didn't know," the farmer said simply, in his native tongue.

"You didn't know a barbwire harness would cut into your donkey's flesh?" she retorted, almost losing her cool.

Embarrassed and caught out, the farmer simply shrugged.

"I realize money is tight," she said calmly. "And you're not the only one around here who does this kind of thing, but if you don't look after your animals properly it'll cost you more to replace them than if you had looked after them in the first place."

"Yes, miss."

Charlene sighed, and headed to her jeep. Painted on the door was: *Zimbabwe National SPCA: Chief Inspector, Charlene*

Tynsworth. She tossed the farmer's barbwire harness into the back of her jeep and reached inside to find a new leather one. Assuming they were heading home, Shaka jumped onto the front passenger's seat.

"Not yet, boy. Soon," she smiled.

With a heavy sigh, Charlene handed over the leather harness to the farmer. "Promise me you'll use this from now on."

"Yes, miss. I promise."

Nuzzling into her touch, the donkey felt the warmth, love and devotion of this special woman, enjoying her affectionate caress, when suddenly, loud gunshots filled the air. They all looked around to see where the noise came from.

"Oh no," she gasped.

Bursting through the brush, a terrified wounded leopard panted her escape from pursuing armed hunters and their packs of ferocious collared hounds. The collars were remote-controlled and electrified. If any hound dared chase after the wrong species it was soon punished for its efforts. The lowest setting of the electric collars caused mere pain, but the higher settings caused vomiting, and if inflicted often enough could break a dog's back, causing an agonizing death. It was an extremely efficient method of keeping hunting hounds under control and on the right scent.

The leopard had seen this all before, but she'd never before been at the sharp end of a hunt. Over her three years on this earth the precious spotted cat had seen lion, cheetah and caracal chased to exhaustion and then slaughtered by the two-legs, the most fearsome and brutal of all the predators in the jungle. It had always been something of a mystery to the leopard as to why this predator hunted the wildlife of Africa – they didn't seem to be hungry, in fact many of them seemed disproportionately large for their basic construction. And the animals they hunted never appeared to be posing a threat of any kind to them. No, the two-legs were just opportunistic killers, striking out at any species they came across for reasons that clearly had nothing whatever to do with the creator's rules of survival. But right now, the reasons weren't important. The two-legs and their hounds were after her.

She was outnumbered, injured and worn out, but she had to run and keep running, for her very life depended on it.

She noticed the two-legs were carrying a foreign object: something the creator had not seen fit to give them at birth. It was a long stick-like object that made a loud noise, and whenever the loud noise happened some animal always fell down wounded, generally never to rise again. It was an uneven chase, an unfair mismatch of hunter and hunted. Whenever the leopard hunted it was for food and, equipped only with what nature had given her, as often as not she was unsuccessful in her hunt. But the two-legs seemed never to fail in killing whatever they had set their sights on.

Laughing with adrenalin-pumped sadistic pleasure, half a dozen overweight foreign hunters dressed in army fatigues chased after their hounds. The dogs barked with the infectious blood-lusting frenzy of their masters as they continued to chase and corner the leopard.

The beautiful giant spotted cat was soon overpowered by the hounds who enthusiastically began to tear at her flesh, just as Laurie Watson caught up with the group. Laurie was as tough and mean a son-of-a-bitch as God had ever put on earth. After having been dishonorably discharged from the elite forces of Her Majesty's Special Air Service, he'd soon found a way to make a lucrative living from his expert training. He now ran Matupula Hunting Lodge in Bulawayo. Over the twenty years he'd been in Zimbabwe his British accent had been replaced with the harsh clipped accent of his adopted land. His skin was rough and wrinkled, but his eyes were still piercingly bright blue, and cold as a blade of steel.

"Hey! Stop that! Get them off! They'll ruin the skin!" he ordered his dogs.

Assisted by his native workers, Laurie managed to remove the bloodthirsty hounds off the mortally wounded leopard in time for his customers, the hunters, to gloat over the prize.

"Is it dead?" asked one of the hunters, in a broad Southern American accent.

"Not yet," Laurie replied. "Soon. No point damaging the hide further with a bullet."

Cautiously leering over his prize, the hunter grinned to himself. He didn't notice the wounded leopard's six-month-old cub observing from a distance, confused and panicked.

The cub peered from beneath blades of grass, which to the infant towered as high as an impenetrable fortress. She cocked her head to one side, trying to get a grasp of what was happening to her mother. Why didn't she just come home? The cub was hungry and sensed a descending coldness from the falling dusk. She yearned for the warmth and security of mother. Unable to contain her anguish, the cub cried out.

"Shit," Laurie spat.

"What?" a hunter asked.

"There's a cub."

"So?"

"So we're not supposed to kill nursing mothers."

"That's easily fixed," the hunter leered, reloading a cartridge into his rifle. "We wouldn't wanna leave the little bastard out here an orphan, now would we?"

Laurie smiled his agreement.

The light was fading in the mother leopard's eyes, but she wasn't dead yet. Although she didn't speak their tongue, she understood all too well what they were planning to do. They wanted to kill her baby, her legacy to the creator, her offering to keep her species alive and perpetuating. She could not let that happen. She used her last ounce of strength to raise her head and give her baby a determined "save yourself" glare.

Trying hard to understand what was happening the cub paced back and forth in confusion.

The hunter lined up the cub and squeezed back slowly on the trigger. But before the deadly bullet could hit its mark, the mother leopard lashed out with her claws, tearing into the hunter's calf and causing him to miss his target.

The bullet hit the dirt only inches from the cub. She bounded away like greased lightning.

Screaming in agony, the hunter fell to the ground, while Laurie finished off the mother leopard with a thud from the butt of his rifle. "Cunning bitch."

Turning to examine the hunter, Laurie was relieved to see he'd only received a flesh wound. "Come on, mate. It's not that bad, up you get."

"Not that bad? Look at me! I'm bleeding!"

"You'll live. Come on, we've got an orphan to catch!" Turning to his native workers, Laurie added, "Release the hounds! Get it lads!"

The dogs charged after the terrified cub as it zigzagged its way through the undergrowth. She was young and strong, but inexperienced and terrified. It didn't take long for the highly trained hounds to force her into a clearing, where she discovered with horror she had run straight into an ambush.

Knowing the prey was surrounded, the hounds pounced on the infant like sharks in a feeding frenzy. The cub struck back, inflicting surprisingly deep wounds on her yelping foes. But needles of hot saliva had already penetrated her flesh. She felt dizzy misery and merciless pain as all sense of location became blurred around her.

Without warning, a flash of black lightning suddenly burst out of the bushes. The native farmer Charlene had just helped with his donkey appeared with a rifle slung over his shoulder, brandishing a long wooden walking stick. He pounded at the dogs with the stick, soon forcing them to turn tail and flee. Not satisfied they wouldn't return, the farmer disappeared after them yelling obscenities at the top of his lungs and waving the stick threateningly.

The cub collapsed under a shrub, unable to move now even when her self-preservation instincts told her there was a two-leg standing over her. Leaves rustled with movement. Charlene's face appeared, stained with tears.

"Oh. My poor baby," she sobbed.

Reaching into her knapsack, Charlene pulled out a needle and carefully injected painkiller into the panting cub. "There you go, you'll be alright. Where's your mommy?"

"Well, if it ain't mother nature," Laurie snapped sharply.

Charlene whipped around to see her nemesis standing there with the wounded, sweaty-faced hunter.

"I might have known you were behind this," she shot back.

"Not me, luvvy. You won't find one of my bullets on that carcass."

"She's not dead yet, no thanks to you! But she would have been if I hadn't had got here before your dogs finished her off!"

"You can't seriously believe that I'm responsible for my dogs' actions. They're animals and this is the jungle. They're only doing what God created them to do."

"Give it a rest, Laurie. You know just as well as I do your dogs only attack what you tell them to! Otherwise you wouldn't need those electric shock collars! You're both going to pay for this!"

The hunter's expression dropped instantly, wondering what sort of lawsuit might be brought against him for hunting a nursing mother leopard.

"Is that so?" Laurie replied with deep sarcasm. "Well, considering you seem to know the law so well, you must also realize that I am quite within my rights to shoot you where you stand for trespassing."

With cold hatred in his eyes, Laurie raised his rifle in Charlene's direction.

"You think I'm afraid of you? Pull that trigger, if you've got the guts, and see what happens! I can see the headlines now!"

Laurie lowered his weapon, and Charlene silently let out a sigh of relief.

"If you could really get rid of me that easily, you wouldn't have tried so hard to make all your other attempts look like accidents, would you?"

"I have no idea what you're talking about."

Standing up defiantly, Charlene cradled the injured cub, glaring at Laurie.

"Hey! Where do you think you're going?" the hunter asked, now raising his own rifle at her.

"Put that away," Laurie ordered.

"No!" the hunter protested. "That cub's mine! I want to stuff it for my baby girl's bedroom!"

"I said, put your gun down!" Laurie repeated.

"Why? I shot its mother! It belongs to me!"

"Because, unlike you, *he* will shoot to kill," Laurie replied.

"Who?" the hunter asked, confused.

"Him," Laurie answered, pointing away from Charlene.

Following Laurie's gaze, the hunter quickly saw the farmer had returned and had his own rifle pointed at them.

"Drop your weapons. Drop them!" the farmer ordered, in his native tongue.

Not prepared to take his chances, the hunter nervously, angrily and carefully lowered his rifle to the ground and stepped back from it.

"Okay, now do as I do and walk away slowly," Laurie advised his client.

Terrified, the hunter did exactly as he was told.

"Your hand guns too," Charlene added.

Glaring angrily, Laurie slowly unstrapped his pistol holster and dropped it to the ground.

"Now get the hell out of here before my friend loses his patience." Charlene tried to sound intimidating.

"You've gone too far this time, Charlene," Laurie growled, before storming into the bush with the hunter.

Feeling weak at the knees, Charlene gratefully turned to her rescuer. "Thank you."

The farmer just grinned broadly, displaying a row of dazzling white teeth as he picked up his newly acquired weapons.

"Come on, let's get you fixed up, my baby," she said to the barely conscious cub she was still cradling.

As they turned to head back to Charlene's jeep, a breathtakingly beautiful sunset of fire-red and orange descended on the African horizon, as ants ran up and down a nearby tree.

Chapter 2

Looking down from the network news chopper, the cars on the LA Freeway seemed to resemble the scurrying of busy teeming ants. The midday sun illuminated the iconic "Hollywood" sign through a smog-filled glary skyline. In Beverly Hills, roller-bladers skated, dog-lovers walked their poodles, and yuppies drove their high-performance sports cars past shops that displayed fake leopard-print merchandise ranging from furniture to fashion.

Striding down Rodeo Drive in a stunning white outfit, sun hat and glasses, Paula Gooding carried armfuls of designer bags. She stopped to check her reflection in a shop window. She looked barely thirty, with perfect skin and a body to match. Her golden hair ruffled slightly in the gentle breeze, but otherwise there wasn't a speck out of place on this 'designer legend'.

She stopped outside a monument to capitalism: an art gallery shop-front of chrome and glass that sparkled in the morning sun. She looked at the etching displaying the establishment's name, *Gooding's Art Gallery,* and sighed, remembering the responsibility for keeping it going was all hers.

Inside the huge two-story open-plan gallery, a large array of paintings were displayed on every wall and up an ornate marble horseshoe staircase. Philippe Dante, Paula's overtly gay, thirty-something assistant and best friend, locked a safety deposit box and placed it in a wall safe behind his meticulously clean desk.

"'Morning, Philippe," Paula chirped, entering the gallery.

He spun around to face her. "Morning? More like afternoon."

"I know, I'm so sorry. I totally forgot we had that big auction this morning."

"What do I care? You're the boss."

"How did it go?"

"We made a killing, as usual."

"Oh, Philippe. What would I do without you?"

"Let me think ... well, you'd have to do everything, now wouldn't you?"

"Don't remind me," she huffed, leaning heavily against the front entry desk. She took off her sunglasses and rubbed her eyes.

"Still depressed I see," Philippe quipped. "Retail therapy with Doctor Gucci didn't help?"

"It's no good. Why do I feel like my whole world is crushing in around me? I need something to do. I mean really *do*."

"Don't tell me the material girl is finally growing a conscience?"

"If that's your best attempt at cheering me up, don't bother."

"Oh, honey, I didn't mean it like that. I only meant that most people live out their whole lives without realizing they ought to give something back, rather than just take, take, taking. Hey, wait a minute." He shuffled through his in-tray. "Let's see. I think I received an invitation to an Animal Welfare Seminar only yesterday - from an organization the gallery sometimes donates to."

"We do?" Paula asked, surprised. She was quite happy to donate to charity, but she felt somewhere inside her that if she was doing something philanthropic she should at least be aware, so she could feel good about it.

"Of course," Philippe answered matter-of-factly. "Every time the gallery does particularly well, I donate a small percentage of the profits to various tax-deductible causes."

Paula's eyes widened; clearly clueless about her own business.

"Ah! Here we go," he announced. "Two VIP invites to the African Wildlife Protection information seminar. I had thought of taking a hot date, but I suppose you'll have to do."

"Thanks a lot," she sniffed, taking the invitations. "I didn't know you were an animal lover."

"I'm not really. I mean, I hate any kind of cruelty whether it be against man or beast. But that's not the reason I was going."

"Then why?"

"It's run by Joan Taylor - you know, from all those Hitchcock films. Who knows, I may get some hot goss on Hitchcock, or better yet, I might get to meet her hunky son!"

"And here I was thinking you were doing this to teach *me* not to be so shallow."

"Hey, I know I'm shallow, but I don't have a problem with it. You do. So you wanna go, or not?"

"What have I got to lose?" she shrugged. "You know, I feel better already. Have you had lunch?"

"What do you think?"

"Come on then. My treat."

Turning around, Paula tried to get the attention of the gallery's girl Friday, Lisa Mendoza. In her early thirties, Lisa had come from south of the border to make her fame and fortune in Hollywood. Looking like a Spanish porn-queen, she couldn't understand why no one had snapped her up yet as the latest and greatest starlet to hit Sunset Boulevard. She positively oozed sex appeal and she knew it. Unfortunately for her, her aversion to work of any sort, and her "the world owes me a living" attitude, didn't do her any favors when it came to job interviews, let alone auditions.

"Excuse me, Lisa," Paula called, noticing her staff member was once again reading some trashy magazine. "Would you mind watching the gallery for a couple of hours?"

Lisa sighed heavily, not welcoming the interruption to the juicy article she was reading, and not welcoming the fact that the article wasn't about her in the first place. "Si, Madam Gooding, not a problem," she replied, reluctantly.

"Remind me again why we hired her," Paula whispered to Philippe.

"You remember?" he hissed. "The day she came in to offer her services, the clientele seemed to hang around a lot longer and spend a lot more."

Lisa seductively sauntered up to a middle-aged customer as if to prove the point, right on cue.

"Oh yes," Paula murmured.

"Who knows? If you're nice to her, she may show us both how to attract Mr. Right."

HAVING MARCHED INTO the highly polished wooden office of the Minister for National Parks and Wildlife in Zimbabwe, Charlene threw the carcass of the dead leopard cub on a large mahogany desk. The Minister stared with unsympathetic eyes. This hardly surprised Charlene. On the wall behind him a stuffed leopard sat perched on a tree limb as if it were still alive and about to pounce on its prey.

"If a local farmer did this, he'd be thrown in jail and have his dogs destroyed!" she shouted.

"That's an entirely different matter," the Minister replied robotically.

"Because locals don't have American dollars? Even the CEO of the Hunting Association here objects to these barbaric hunting methods!"

"I'm afraid even *his* objections are not loud enough to balance an annual revenue of seventy million American dollars."

"You know as well as I do there are no up-to-date stats on leopard numbers in Zim. You're selling off our wildlife for thirty pieces of silver. At the rate you're allowing them to be slaughtered, there'll be none left in ten years."

"Make that five years, Miss Tynsworth," he replied with cold candor.

Charlene's jaw fell open in amazement. He wasn't even trying to pretend what they were doing was wrong. "And what then?" she asked.

The Minister just shrugged, as if to say, "Who cares?"

"Well, you might be prepared to sit back and do nothing, but I'm not!"

"And what exactly do you propose to do?"

"You expect me to give you my game plan so you can get your cronies stop me? Do I look that stupid?"

He looked at her as if to say, "Well, if you're not that stupid, what are you doing here in the first place?"

She understood all too well that she was wasting her time and stormed out. Almost frustrated to tears, she returned to her jeep, which was parked in a dusty car park near the Minister's office in Harare.

Leaning cross-armed against a flimsy wooden fence, Laurie stood patiently waiting for her. He knew she'd head straight to the Minister to complain about his activities, and while he suspected what the reaction would be, he needed to be certain.

"Oh, boohoo, a little leopard got killed," he called tauntingly.

Charlene kept walking.

"'Big deal!' That's what he told you, didn't he? He couldn't care less as long as I keep lining his pockets, could he?"

Charlene froze on the spot, took a huge intake of air, then spun around to face the man she saw as the Devil incarnate. "Someone will care," she assured him.

Getting the bite he wanted, Laurie decided to stalk his prey. "I'm simply a businessman supplying a demand. If it wasn't me, it would be someone else."

Charlene breathed hard, her eyes blazing with rage.

"It's obvious you and I are never going to agree on this," Laurie said calmly. "But I'm not an unreasonable man. How's about we come to an arrangement that suits everyone?"

"Please explain how anything you do will ever suit me."

"Forget the animals for one minute, will you? I'm offering you a solution."

"You scratch my back, I scratch yours, huh?"

"Exactly."

"A bribe? There isn't enough money in the world to stop me exposing every last one of you bastards!"

She turned back to her jeep and climbed in. Not satisfied that his point had been made, Laurie leant menacingly in her open driver's side window.

"Who the hell do you think you are to judge me? You love animals; I love shooting them! Who's to say who's right and who's wrong?"

Charlene tried to put her keys in the ignition, but Laurie reached in and stopped her.

"You wanna see a leopard? Go to a fucking zoo! Or better still, a museum. I probably put them both in there."

Disgusted, Charlene tried again to start her vehicle, but Laurie fixed his cold gaze directly in her eyes, grabbing her wrist so she was unable to start the ignition.

"Hey, I'll even send you a freshly stuffed one from my taxidermist – you can stare at it all day if you like. But don't you ever, EVER, try and tell me what I can and can't do on my own land again! Okay?"

Pulling out of his grip, Charlene defiantly returned Laurie's glare as she turned over her jeep's engine and revved up to leave.

"Excuse me, Laurie, but I have something worthwhile to do with my time." Reversing hard, Charlene forced Laurie to back away.

"That was your last chance, Charlene. I'd watch my back if I were you."

Crunching through the gears, Charlene slammed her jeep into first and prepared to leave, but not before getting in the final shot.

"So it's business as usual, eh Laurie?"

With that she floored it, leaving Laurie to furiously eat dust.

TWO WEEKS LATER, Charlene was back in her home town of Los Angeles, addressing a packed audience in the ballroom of the Los Angeles Hilton. She'd put on a suit for the occasion. It was suffocating her. As she looked out across the sea of well-coiffured hairstyles and dumbstruck faces, she wondered if accepting Joan's offer to address this symposium was really worth taking time away from her hands-on work in Zimbabwe. But Joan had convinced her that if she would just speak to people – real time, in the flesh, fresh with first-hand experiences – she might, just might begin to get some much needed help. It was worth a try anyway.

Although she was accustomed to isolation, and dressing for the bush, and fighting deadly foes who could make her disappear in a heartbeat, she took the podium and addressed the large gathering as though she'd been doing it all her life. Speaking with astonishing confidence and resolve, Charlene outlined a few hard facts and figures.

"With over thirty-five thousand members worldwide, Hunters Inc. claim there are eleven million big game hunters in the United States alone. This is an alarming fact considering there aren't eleven million big game left in the world. In fact, eighty percent of Zimbabwe's wildlife has already been destroyed."

A notice board standing behind Charlene read:

The African Wildlife Protection Foundation, in conjunction with Hollywood Screen Legend "Joan Taylor", presents Acclaimed Conservationist "Charlene Tynsworth".

"And it's not just endangered species that are being brutalized," Charlene continued. "Live bait, such as donkeys and goats, are often left tied to a tree where they are nibbled alive by scavengers for days before the predators find them."

Gruesome slides depicting the situation flashed on a large screen above Charlene's head.

"Another disturbing fact is that none of these hunters are required to undergo any kind of proficiency tests. They are often such bad shots that they couldn't hit water if they fell out of a boat."

The audience laughed. This hadn't been Charlene's intention.

"What this means is," she feverishly tried to get their attention focused back on the matter at hand, "that the initial shot is rarely fatal; the animals usually die in agony."

The audience fell into an embarrassed silence. Good, she thought, in temporary triumph.

"Weapons that have recently been adopted are designed to minimize damage to the trophy, and maximize excitement for the hunter, unlike conventional hunting equipment. Hand guns and bows with barbed arrows are favorites among this group."

Slides above her head flashed on screen showing horrific injuries from these armaments.

"Then there's also the issue of canned hunting, the cowardly practice of shooting an animal while it's captive in a cage. Some big cats are even inbred specifically for this purpose, and often their cubs are present as a dozen slugs are pumped into their mother while she roars in agony for help!"

Taking a moment, Charlene paused to control her emotions.

"Just as an example of these hunters' disregard for the law, let me tell you a story about Botswana. Shortly after its government put in place a ban to protect its own declining lion population, Hunters Inc. petitioned the country to overturn it. Not because they disbelieved the statistics; simply because they wanted to continue hunting lions regardless. Two of the key signatories to that petition were a former American General and a former President of the United States!"

Murmurs of disgust and shock rose from the audience.

"That's the kind of political clout and financial muscle we're up against, and that's why we need your help."

For the following thirty minutes she continued ardently trying to persuade the audience that there were greater things in the world to worry about than whether you were seen in the right restaurant last night. When she finished, to her astonishment she was given a standing ovation.

Clapping madly, with tears in her eyes, Paula hurriedly pushed forward through the crowd to get to Charlene, Philippe scuttling along closely behind her.

"Ms Tynsworth? Ms Tynsworth!" Paula called out. "I had to meet you, I thought what you said was wonderful!"

"Wonderful!?" Charlene gasped. "I would hardly call anything I had to say *wonderful*."

"Oh, I know," Paula gushed. "I just meant your passion for these animals is awe-inspiring."

"These poor creatures need more than our passion if they're going to survive."

"Well that's why we're here. We would love to help your cause, it's just ..."

"Let me guess. Your hands are tied," Charlene scoffed.

Before Paula could explain, a voice from behind her intervened. "Well, let's untie them."

Spinning around, Paula saw Joan Taylor standing there, large as life.

"Joan, Ms Taylor," she corrected herself. "It's an honor to meet you. I'm Paula Gooding." Blushing like a schoolgirl, Paula shot out her hand.

"Hello, Paula," Joan replied, amused but gracious.

"And this is my assistant and good friend, Philippe Dante."

"Pleased to meet you." Joan offered Philippe her hand.

"Charmed, Ms Taylor," Philippe replied, slithering his hand into hers. "Forgive me for asking, but what was it really like working with Hitch?"

"Philippe!" Paula hissed.

"That's alright," Joan smiled. "It was the most amazing experience of my life. But I'm more interested in what Paula was trying to say earlier, than talking about my past."

"What I was trying to say," Paula smiled at Philippe, "was I would love to help your cause, I just don't know where to start. What exactly do you need?"

"Money!" Charlene and Joan replied as one.

"Well, that's something I can confidently say we know quite a bit about," Philippe quipped back.

"Well then," Joan answered. "Perhaps we should find somewhere where we can have a quiet chat."

Charlene kept her expression stone-faced. She'd heard it all before and it never amounted to anything. But if Joan wanted to talk to these two gushing sycophants, well, she didn't have anything better to do with the rest of the night.

Joan led the way, smiling and shaking hands with potential donors as they gradually trudged through the crowd and made it to a quiet corner table in the a la carte restaurant of the hotel. Having settled in, ordered four vegetarian meals, and taken breath over a glass or two of claret, Joan, Paula and Philippe sat back to listen to Charlene explain what they could do to *really* make a difference.

"To get the proof we need we'd have to hire someone to infiltrate the hunting group at Matupula. These hunters are mega-rich and politically powerful – finding someone able to expose them won't come cheap."

"Why don't you just go to the media?" Paula asked.

"The networks won't even attempt to touch it without some kind of visual evidence first," Joan explained.

"You take the risk, they get the glory?" Philippe asked rhetorically.

"Exactly," Joan agreed.

"Forgive me for asking, Joan, but you're a movie star. Couldn't you afford to fund the undercover operation yourself?" Paula flushed even as she asked the question, but it seemed a reasonable question to ask.

"I'd love nothing more, but I have to raise close to a million dollars a year just to keep my own preserve going."

Paula instantly sank back with embarrassment.

"I have sixty-three big cats and an elephant in my care," Joan explained. "I am solely responsible for funding their food, shelter, vet bills - you name it. I wonder everyday where I'm going to get the money from. I never wonder *if*, but every day I wonder *how*."

"I see. Well, maybe we could organize a fundraiser?" Paula suggested. "You know, an African-themed Gala Night. I'm sure with a profile like yours they'll be lining up to attend."

"That sounds like a great idea," Joan agreed.

"Really?" Paula puffed with pride.

"Sure. You organize it and I'll be there," Joan smiled.

"Me?" Paula spluttered. "Oh no. I wouldn't have any idea about what it takes to run a charity event."

"Just spread the news through the LA grapevine that you're trying to raise funds to save endangered animals. Use my name."

"Oh! I'd love to but…"

Star-struck at the possibilities, Philippe couldn't contain himself. "When do we start?"

"Philippe!" Paula nudged him.

"What? Come on, Paula! It'll be a blast! I even know an investigative journalist who might be interested in the secret spy mission."

"You do?" Paula asked, shocked.

"Ex-boyfriend. I'll give him a call."

Joan smiled at the banter. She had a good feeling about the art gallery owner and her colorful friend. "What do you think, Charlene?"

Charlene looked a bit overwhelmed for a moment. "To be blatantly honest, I don't care how we expose this racket, as long as what we're trying to do doesn't leave this table. If anyone gets wind of the real reason for the fundraiser, it could endanger all our lives."

Philippe shuddered.

"Do you understand?" Charlene challenged him.

"Perfectly," Paula and Philippe answered together.

"Good. Then it looks like you've got a busy time ahead of you, doesn't it?" Joan cheered, fishing into her pocketbook and pulling out a business card. "When you have questions, or need help, and you will, give me a call."

"I CAN'T BELIEVE I allowed myself to get talked into this," Paula berated herself, pacing the gallery.

"Will you relax?" Philippe sighed melodramatically. "I'm doing all the ringing around. All you have to do is supply the venue, look stunning and claim the credit!"

"You'll get your share of back slapping."

"And bum slapping too, I hope."

"You're incorrigible."

"Only when you encourage me, darling."

As they giggled to themselves, a slightly built Indian man in an offensively tacky orange suit walked into the gallery. Philippe eyed him up and down, first with distaste, then like a hungry cat might eye a passing mouse.

"Well hello," Philippe mewed. "How can we help you today?"

Nudging him in the ribs, Paula signaled to Philippe to cool down the "campness", which was obviously making the visitor uncomfortable.

"My name is Harbens Punjarb. I'm an artist," the man offered, lifting a portfolio up to the counter and continuing his obviously well-rehearsed spiel.

Philippe rolled his eyes at Paula. If there was one thing he - they - didn't need right now it was *another* would-be artist trying to get Gooding's Art Gallery to display his work.

"I've admired your gallery for many years," Harbens continued, undeterred. "But when I heard about the fundraiser, I felt compelled to offer my services."

"We're grateful for any help. Go on," Paula urged.

Opening his portfolio, Harbens displayed photos of his work. Paula and Philippe both gawped in amazement. His work was quite fabulous. The detailed brushwork, the use of color, and the obvious passion for his subject matter had enabled Harbens to produce some remarkable canvasses. There was no doubt about it - the man was gifted.

"Though I was born in India, my family and I lived in Africa for many years before moving to the States. As you can see from my work, I have a deep love for Africa's wildlife."

"There is no denying you're very talented. But considering you're an unknown in LA, I can't quite see how you can help us," Philippe said reluctantly.

"I thought you might be interested in auctioning off some of my work at your Gala if I were to offer, say, fifty percent of all sales to your Fund?"

Paula looked toward Philippe who shrugged in response.

"That's a very generous offer," Paula conceded.

"Well, considering the cause, a… and the possible exposure it might create for me, I'm prepared to make the sacrifice."

"Alright, Mr. Punjarb! You've got yourself a deal," Paula cheered.

Harbens vigorously shook her hand in reply, happening to notice Lisa staring at him from the other side of the gallery like a hungry animal. She seductively pouted her lips and blew him a kiss. He forced his gaze away, hoping neither Paula nor Philippe had noticed.

"Yes, well, this is all very nice, but Paula darling, don't you have an appointment you're already late for?" Philippe asked.

"Oh my sainted aunt," Paula gasped, looking at her Rolex. "I'm sorry, Mr Punjarb. I really have to fly. But it's been very nice meeting you. And thank you. I'm very grateful. It's a very generous offer. You won't regret it. I – "

"Oh, go already!" Philippe shouted, in mock anger.

"Of course," Paula flustered. "Well, I'll see you later." With that she flew out of the gallery, leaving her bag and car keys behind. Philippe grabbed them and stood there holding them in one hand, while resting his other hand melodramatically on his hip. A heartbeat later Paula breezed back into the gallery, grabbed her bag and keys from Philippe, gave him a kiss on the forehead, smiled embarrassedly at Harbens, and flew out again.

JERRY'S DELI on Beverly Boulevard was always packed with patrons, no matter what time of the day or night. Conveniently situated right in the middle of the area where every Hollywood agent had an office, the Deli's menu featured something from just about every corner of the globe. Service was always prompt and with a smile. With such a constant hubbub it was paradoxically the perfect place to have a covert meeting – no one was likely to overhear a word that was said on a neighboring table.

Alone in a secluded booth, Paula twiddled her straw in a glass of mineral water, scanning the buzzing crowd. As she looked around, a ruggedly good-looking man strode confidently in from the right, with an air of having 'seen it all before'. He was wearing mirrored sunglasses, but in Hollywood that was nothing unusual, even in the dimmed light of the deli. He stopped for a moment, scanned the crowd like a predator and made a beeline for Paula.

"Hello there," he said, very sure of himself.

Stunned by his boldness, Paula blushed. "Er, hi."

"You must be Paula."

Tilting her own sunglasses down, Paula couldn't help but flirt with this handsome man. "Do I know you?"

"Philippe sent me."

"Oh? Oh! You're Tom Green!" Now she *really* blushed.

"That's right."

"How did you know who I was?"

"I wouldn't be much of an investigative reporter if I didn't, now would I?"

Paula stared at him. Philippe had said the person he would introduce her to, the one who could help with the covert mission, was "an ex-boyfriend". Studying every pulsing muscle in Tom's perfectly formed body (even through his clothes) Paula couldn't quite believe she had heard that right.

"Are you okay?" Tom asked.

"Sure. Yes. Sorry. It's just - you don't seem Philippe's - er - type."

Tom sat down, unmoved. "I'm guessing you didn't invite me here to talk about my sexual preferences?"

"Of course. I mean, of course not." Damn, she felt like a bumbling schoolgirl, and here she was about to talk about some secret under-cover covert James Bond mission. What a twit she felt.

Tom brushed off her faux pas with a cheeky smile and pulled out a well-worn leather-bound notepad which he thumbed through.

"After Philippe's call, I did a bit of research on Hunters Inc. It seems you're not the first to try and expose them."

"Really?"

"A couple of years ago a British reporter almost smuggled out some incriminating footage. He ended up being brutalized and thrown out of the country for his efforts."

"Oh my God," she paused. "What are you trying to say? That the job's impossible?"

"Oh no, it's possible alright."

She sighed with relief. "Then you'll do it?"

"Absolutely not."

"What? I thought you just said ... Well why? I mean, why not?"

"This is way out of my league," Tom explained calmly.

"But Philippe told me you spend most of your time working in war-torn countries. Surely this is no more dangerous than that?"

"I'd rather be in a war zone any day than take on these guys."

"So you can't help us?"

"Not personally. But I may be able to organize a meeting for you with some men who could, if you're really serious about this."

"I am. I've never been more serious about anything in my life. Come to think of it, I don't think I've ever been serious about anything in my life – until now."

"I wouldn't usually pass on information like this, but if Philippe says he trusts you, then I hope I can trust you. And if I trust you, so will my contacts."

“I’m intrigued. Who are these men?”

Chapter 3

Heavy rain poured over lush green foliage in the Colombian jungle. The thundering precipitation was so loud it made it almost impossible to hear anything above the deluge that exploded all around. It was as if Mother Nature's wrath was being released to wreak revenge with the full fury of a woman scorned. It was both a blessing and a curse for the camouflaged ex-special forces team that had taken up position on a hill above a valley clearing.

As Tom sat in the warmth and comfort of Jerry's Deli in Los Angeles, explaining to Paula, "They're a group of former special forces operatives, now operating 'semi-privately'", with a single hand signal, team leader Brendan "Bricks" Mackenzie caused his whole team to drop to the ground.

"CIA, FBI, SAS, DEA. You name it they've got an initial for it. And your little mission is right up their alley," Tom explained to Paula in Los Angeles, while in Colombia, team leader Bricks Mackenzie pointed to his eyes then made a circular gesture and a downward fist, signaling his team to move in.

Beneath the Colombian hill, a group of guerillas took cover from the rain under a tent by a small peasant shanty.

Spying through his binoculars, second-in-command Vernon O'Brien assessed the situation, reporting back into his headset radio.

"Eagle Eye to Foxhole, I have visual contact. Five men at twelve o'clock, and four at nine o'clock. Over."

"How many inside?" Bricks called back.

"Unknown," Vernon replied.

"Do you have the target in sight?"

“Negative. Wait!”

Suddenly the guerilla leader, a huge man with a grotesquely bulging belly, dragged a peasant out into the rain, pistol-whipped him, then aimed the gun at his head. The peasant knelt, pressing his hands together in supplication, begging for his life. The leader wrenched his head back and shoved the barrel of the gun into the peasant’s mouth, ignoring pleas from his family who were fearfully following outside.

Disgusted at what he was witnessing, Vernon pulled out his own weapon and took aim through his sniper rifle sight.

The leader squeezed the trigger. CLICK. Nothing happened. Laughing hysterically, the leader stepped back to watch the peasant fall to the ground in shock.

Turning to his men, the leader did a little victory dance in the rain, which seemed to cause much amusement in the ranks. The peasant’s family in turn ran crying to the fallen man’s aid.

“See what could happen without our protection?” the leader yelled in Spanish. “You should be thanking us that we camp near your homes. Now if I hear one more complaint from any of you - ” The leader slid a magazine into his pistol, “Bam, Bam, Bam, Bam!” He clicked the safety back on.

From his vantage point, Vernon breathed a sigh of relief.

Slipping and sliding in the mud, and drenched from the rain, the peasants helped each back into their home, as the leader unveiled a crate of cheap whisky from under a tarpaulin. Spinning the bottles through the air, he tossed one each to his men who happily accepted the offering and disappeared into their tents to get drunk.

The leader slapped the peasant’s daughter on her backside as she passed him, laughing to himself at his absolute power over this dominion.

“Do you have the shot?” Bricks called into his headset to Vernon.

With the crosshair dead on target, Vernon aimed for the leader’s head. “Affirmative.”

“Then drop him and let’s get the hell out of here,” Bricks ordered.

Squeezing the trigger, Vernon hesitated and softened his grip.

"What are you waiting for?" Bricks barked.

"The contract stated dead or alive. If I can extract the target alive, I wanna try," Vernon explained.

"Are you out of your freaking mind? Take the shot and we'll be over the border before they know what hit them."

"I can do this," Vernon insisted.

"Forget what the contract says! We're here to neutralize a known terrorist."

Ignoring his senior officer, Vernon made his way to the enemy's camp with the stealth of a black panther. Bricks was on the scene in heartbeat, with fellow commando Jackson Anderson.

"What's he doing?" Jackson asked.

"Going soft," Bricks scowled.

Sneaking past the guerrillas' tents, Vernon could only see their silhouettes as they laughed and drank. Checking that the coast was clear, he carefully crept up behind the relaxed leader. Striking like a cobra, Vernon grabbed the leader and shoved a rag in his mouth.

The leader tried to reach for his pistol but was out cold before he stood a chance. Vernon slapped a pair of handcuffs on him then rubbed smelling salts under his nose. The leader's eyes snapped open to the sight of a razor-sharp blade at his throat and Vernon gesturing to him that "he'd better keep quiet".

Nodding his fearful agreement, the leader silently stood and let Vernon drag him away.

"Slick bastard," Jackson muttered to Bricks.

Vernon was halfway across the muddy road when a truckload of Colombian soldiers came bouncing over the uneven ground around the mountain road corner.

"Shit! Get out of there, Vernon!" Bricks ordered.

Before the command could register, the Colombian troops had already opened fire.

Diving to the ground for cover, Vernon used the leader as a shield.

Also taken by surprise, the guerrillas exited their tents firing machine guns.

Bricks and his commandos opened fire to cover Vernon. Daringly dodging gunfire, the second-in-command crossed the muddy chasm between the shanty and the relative safety of his team. They had almost made it when the leader was torn to shreds by crossfire.

Spinning around, Vernon noticed the peasants were outside again with weapons of their own, determined to add their own vengeance to the bloodshed.

At that moment a Colombian soldier spotted the camouflaged commandos. "Up there! Snipers!" the soldier shouted in Spanish.

As the commandos were forced to fight, the battle spread into all-out warfare.

"Go, go, go! Move!" Bricks ordered all his men.

"What are you doing? Pull back. Pull back!" Vernon came back. But his order fell on deaf ears. Sweeping down like birds of prey, the commandos descended on the valley, almost effortlessly eliminating all opposition. Vernon could only look on in horror at the appalling carnage that unfolded.

"Secure the perimeter!" Bricks yelled.

"We got a live one here!" Jackson called back.

Bricks looked down at a badly bleeding peasant.

"Gringo.. Americana?" the peasant asked hopefully.

Bricks pulled out his pistol.

"No!" Vernon yelled to his leader, already knowing he was wasting his breath. He closed his eyes as the fatal bullet hit its mark. At that moment, with violence and adrenalin familiarly pumping through his veins, Vernon actually believed he would be capable of wiping out all remaining life in the area. And that scared him to death. Jackson approached him from behind. Vernon spun, ready to strike.

"Hey, whoa there, big fella. It's me, one of the good guys."

Before anyone could say another word, a large Navy helicopter blocked out what little light remained, its blades whipping noisily through the air as it took position to extract the undercover team. Rope ladders were tossed out and, as if operated by remote control, the covert operatives scrambled up them to head home. Vernon was the last to leave, taking a final scowling look at the appalling loss of life he had just been a party to. Once safely inside he sat with his head in his hands.

"What the hell's wrong with you?" Bricks yelled over the chopper blades. "In case you've forgotten, this isn't American soil. No one was supposed to know we were here."

"It didn't have to go that way," Vernon replied numbly. "They didn't have a clue who we were."

"We couldn't take that chance. Don't forget we're not *officially* working for the government on this one. Just think of the political can of worms it could have opened up. And then you could kiss any further assignments good-bye."

"What about the innocent victims?"

"There are no innocent victims. They're casualties of war."

"But we're not *at* war."

"As long as there are warriors on both sides, we're at war! Don't preach our old rules of engagement to me; they don't apply anymore! The only rule now is, if they push us, we push back harder! That's our job!"

"I left the CIA because of jobs like this!"

"Bullshit! You left because you wanted a bigger slice of the pie!"

"Well not anymore, I'm finished! I'm out!"

"Out? Yeah right. To where?"

Vernon didn't answer.

"That's what I thought. So, I'll see you in the office bright and early Monday morning, eh?"

Bricks was right. Vernon had nowhere else to go. He hated that. Hated that Bricks was right. Hated that he had nowhere else to go. Just for once he wished a job would land in his lap that he could feel proud of doing, instead of feeling a sickening sinking feeling in the dark pit of his stomach when he went home to his empty apartment.

IT WAS A REMARKABLY normal office. Paula had become used to security entrances since 9-11, so the fact that this office required confirmation of the identity of the caller before it opened didn't make it stand out among the many others. Yet she felt nervous. By all accounts - well, by Tom's account - the men she was about to meet were trained killers. That was, she considered, what these ex-special forces types were made up of. Tom had explained that these were the kind of men you called to do a job that no-one else could do. They were experts with weapons, surveillance equipment, counter-intelligence, and they were no strangers to adopting false identities to penetrate whatever it was that needing penetrating to complete a mission.

Double-checking the address written on the card in front of her, Paula compared it with the small nondescript shop front.

Sitting inside behind a huge white desk with a mirrored glass window behind her, a bespectacled middle-aged woman called Margaret checked Paula's ID before buzzing her in.

"Good morning, Ms Gooding," she offered, as Paula stepped tentatively inside.

"Good morning," she answered nervously, looking around for hidden snipers.

"They're expecting you," Margaret smiled. She was quite used to that shell-shocked look among civilian clientele. Most of their clients had been military and police prior to 9-11, but since the terrorist attacks, more and more private individuals were looking for risk-assessment and body-guarding than ever before. It was all they could do to recruit to keep up with demand.

Margaret led Paula through another security door, as a video camera watched their every move. Inside the boardroom, Jackson watched her on a miniature monitor in a pop-up screen in the desk. He zoomed in on Paula's backside.

"Nice ass –" he began, before noticing Vernon glaring at him disapprovingly. "Nice asset," he quipped, just as Margaret brought Paula in.

After basic introductions were out of the way, Paula opened a thin, designer-made briefcase, which seemed to cause Jackson further amusement. She handed them each a file.

Cleaned up, clean-shaven and dressed in dark FBI-style suits, Bricks, Jackson and Vernon all sat silently studying the files while Paula sat stiffly on the other side of the table. She couldn't help noticing how sparse the furniture was; nor could she help noticing the video camera that winked at her from the corner of the ceiling. As the men continued reading, she felt it was safe to have a closer look at each of them. Bricks was square-jawed and built like his name suggested. Jackson's piercing cold blue eyes were expressionless when focused on the job at hand, but teasingly mischievous the moment he switched to 'off-duty' mode. Vernon was another matter. He had an air that seemed somehow different from the other two. There was a paradoxical soft strength about him. His dark brown eyes were soulful but powerful. When he spoke his voice had a deep resonance that was gentle and seductive, yet forceful and threatening at the same time. While he commanded respect in both his stature and his bearing, there was also a heavy sadness about him. He was both intriguing and foreboding.

Suddenly Bricks slid the file back towards Paula. She snapped her attention back to the matter at hand, almost jumping at the forced break in concentration. Bricks registered the reaction silently. The women always went for Vernon.

"The question isn't can we do this. The question is can you afford us and deal with the repercussions once we get this footage?" Bricks looked her squarely in the eye, testing her resolve.

"If you're not prepared to take any risks in life, maybe you don't have anything to lose," she said as confidently as she could. There was no question that she felt intimidated by this man, but she would be damned if she was going to show it.

Vernon hid a smile, admiring her gumption. He glanced at Bricks who understood almost telepathically that it was time for them to discuss the merits of this job – privately. He pressed a button on a speakerphone in the desk.

"Margaret, could you fix our guest a coffee?" Bricks said.

"Yes, sir," Margaret's voice came back over the speaker as clearly as if she was in the room.

Bricks counted out "one, two, three" on his fingers, and right on cue the door opened and Margaret appeared.

"This way, Ms Gooding," Margaret said coolly.

"Oh, no thanks Margaret, I'm fine."

"What Mr. Mackenzie is trying to say is, give us a moment to discuss this in private," Vernon explained.

"Oh. Sorry. Of course," Paula replied, feeling stupid and embarrassed.

As soon as she was out of the room, the debate between the three men was on.

"Well, what do you think?" asked Vernon.

"It can be done," Bricks said simply.

"But do we want to do it?" Jackson added.

"Why wouldn't we?" Vernon wanted to know.

"I doubt we'd be able to charge our normal fees. It's basically a charity job."

"Not everything's about money."

"Bullshit!"

"I say we do it," Vernon announced firmly.

"Why?"

"Why not?"

"Not good enough."

"Okay then, A: Because I want to. B: Because it would be refreshing to do something good for a change. And C: I admire the lady's passion."

"Yeah, she had one sweet pair of passions!" Jackson leered.

Vernon shot another glare of disapproval at his colleague.

"The point is," Bricks interrupted, sighing at the usual and predictable banter, "we're not a charity. And I doubt very much she could even cover our expenses."

"So, I'll go it alone. I've handled solo missions before."

"It's still gonna cost. Fake identities, inside intel, equipment. Not to mention the first-class travel and accommodation you'd need to convince these guys you're a fellow player."

"Forget the money for once in your life, would you?"

"Sorry, Vernon, my decision is final."

"Then I'll offer my service for free."

Neither Jackson nor Bricks could contain their scoffing laughter, until they realized Vernon was deadly serious. He pressed the speakerphone button. "Margaret, send Ms Gooding back in, please."

Bricks dived onto the speakerphone button like a swooping falcon. "Belay that order, Margaret. Give us one more minute."

"Yes, sir."

Bricks shook his head. "Alright, you bloody fool. Have it your way. Just do exactly as I say."

By the time Paula returned to the meeting room, Bricks had already typed up a list of estimated costs from a pop-up console in front of him.

"If you'll press the button in front of you," Bricks said to Paula, "you'll see a rough job outline."

Paula pressed the button and a screen rose out of the desk. Her eyes widened at the impressive technology, causing Jackson to again grin to himself. They widened further when she saw the numbers that were involved, a fact that caused no one amusement.

"I had no idea it would cost this much."

Bricks gave Vernon an "I told you so" look.

"That's only the tip of the iceberg," Jackson announced. "There'll always be unknown extras in a job like this. And we're going to need at least a sixty-five percent deposit before we can commit any assets."

"I'll have my bank wire you the money today," she said firmly.

All three men raised impressed eyebrows at each other.

"Fine," Bricks replied without emotion. "Then sign your life away and from now on you'll liaise directly with Vernon, who will also be your field operative."

She looked at Vernon and smiled, thinking she saw a glimmer of a smile in reply.

"ARE YOU OUT OF your tiny mind?" Philippe yelled, steadying himself against a large bronze statue that had just arrived in the gallery. "When I said you needed to change your life, I didn't mean mine as well! What happens if you don't raise enough to pay back the overdraft? If you lose this gallery it affects all of us!"

"Then we'd better make sure we put on the best fundraiser Hollywood has ever seen."

Philippe feigned a faint behind the statue.

"Oh come on, Philippe. You're the one who got me into this. Get with the program."

"The program?! She wants me to get with the program. Why did I ever open my big mouth? That'll teach me – no good deed ever goes unpunished."

"Have you finished?" she smiled.

"Finished? Darling, I haven't even started!"

OVER THE FOLLOWING weeks, glossy "Africarnival Charity Gala Night" flyers arrived in the gallery and were unceremoniously dumped on the front counter. Philippe busied himself directing various event coordinators and delivery men. Harbens' paintings arrived and were hung in pride of place around the gallery. And every time Philippe looked, Lisa seemed to be arduously engrossed with filing her nails or reading a magazine.

In Zimbabwe, Charlene scanned piles of paper from a battery-powered machine and emailed the information to: pgooding@yahoo.com, via a laptop on satellite link.

Paula spent most of her time in her apartment in Beverly Hills going over maps and plans with Vernon. The event was only a by-product to her – the mission was what really mattered.

As time ticked by, Philippe became more and more 'native', eventually routinely wearing a tribal headdress, as he continued to give orders to the various staff he'd engaged to put the event together. Gooding's Art Gallery was gradually transformed into an African wonderland as themed decorations, props, and plants were all put in place.

Sitting up in her bed, Charlene looked through some newspaper clippings on Laurie and Hunters Inc, wondering if this time she would finally be able to expose these bastards to the world and put a stop to the brutality against the magnificent endangered big game. Lying next to her, upside down and very content, Shaka's only interest was having his belly tickled.

In Vernon's office, Bricks and Jackson took care of the false IDs and associated paperwork Vernon was going to need to successfully pull off his cover story. Passport photos were taken, phone diversions put in place, and pinhole camera equipment checked and double-checked.

Smiling for the cameras, Joan Taylor and Harbens shook hands in front of one of Harbens' magnificent paintings of two zebras fighting. Joan, gracious and elegant as ever, tried to ignore Lisa's constant attempts to slide into the background of the photographs.

With event plans under Philippe's inimitable control, Paula spent more and more time with Vernon getting the finer points of the mission finalized in liaison with Charlene. She was exhausted but exhilarated. The very idea of coordinating this covert mission was the most exciting thing she had ever done, but it was also the most expensive. She'd put everything, financially, on the line for this. Talk about running before you can walk, she thought to herself. But it was all in a good cause and one she believed in more and more as she gradually learned in sickening detail exactly what was at stake here. Besides that, if she was to be honest with herself, she really didn't mind spending time with this rugged man of mystery.

As days turned to weeks and over a month slid by, she felt like the moth that had flown too close to the flame. She was completely, magnetically captivated by Vernon. He was, unfortunately, all business at all times, but she was confident that couldn't last. She'd tried looking professional, homey, sophisticated – nothing had worked. Today she thought she'd try the casual look. Wearing jeans and a T-shirt, she sat cross-legged on her living room floor, pawing over reams of paperwork with her personal spy. As he looked down to study some statistics her eyes softened, the cause and the mission suddenly vanishing in a puff of lustful smoke.

In the art gallery, Lisa was nonchalantly rifling through the office desk when she came across Paula's diary. She began to flick through it when Philippe called for her from upstairs. She butted out a cigarette, waved away the smoke, slipped the diary into her handbag and rushed to Philippe's aid.

PAULA'S PLANS were coming together beautifully. She checked the time: seven o'clock. Right on schedule there was a knock on her front door. Suddenly she felt like a schoolgirl on her first date. She brushed the feeling off as ridiculous and answered the door.

Vernon's jaw nearly hit the floor.

"Good evening," she said casually.

Even though he kept his eyes fixed firmly on hers, he couldn't help noticing the body-hugging, plunging red dress that clung to her entirely desirable body.

"I'm sorry," he nearly stammered. "I was sure we had a business meeting arranged for tonight."

"Oh, we do. I just thought tonight we could meet over dinner. You haven't eaten yet, have you?"

"Well, no."

"Good, then it's all worked out perfectly."

She grabbed her bag, threw Vernon her car keys, and sauntered down the hallway outside her apartment. He watched her every movement, shook his head, pursed his lips, reminded himself he was trained to be in control of all his emotions at all times, and followed where she led.

She'd chosen The Grill on the Alley restaurant, where the power brokers of Los Angeles enjoyed fine cuisine intermingled with high-powered business negotiations. Paula had reserved the finest table for herself and Vernon, not that she was in the least bit hungry, but surely no man would be able to resist the intoxicating cocktail of food, ambience, charm, fine wine, and a woman who had decided she was prepared to do pretty much anything for him.

When they finished their meals, Vernon looked through his notes, while Paula tipsily sipped more wine.

"This Charlene sure knows her stuff. Her intel has been invaluable," Vernon said formally.

"You're all packed and ready to go?"

"Nearly. I just have to pick up my papers, then I fly out first thing Friday morning."

"I wish you could be at the Gala night."

"It's a matter of priorities."

"Considering the whole night is to pay your wages … I should order you to be there!"

"Yes, sir, boss, sir!" He threw her a mock salute and they laughed as if they were old friends. God, this was hard.

"Have you really killed people?" she suddenly asked.

Taken totally by surprise, Vernon's expression dropped.

"I'm sorry. That was a stupid question."

"No. It wasn't. I'm just not sure you'll want the answer."
"So you have?"
"Yes - but they were all bad."
She chuckled. "That was one of my favorite films!"
"What?"
"*True Lies*. Weren't you quoting Arnie?"
"I don't get to see many films."
For a moment she fell into an embarrassed silence.
"You feel out of place here, don't you?" she eventually asked him softly.
"A little."
"Me too."
"I find that hard to believe."
"Well it's true. I never felt like I fit in."
"You own an art gallery on Rodeo Drive. How much more 'fit in' could you be?"
"Only because I inherited it. If Philippe hadn't stayed on to help me run it, I'd be broke."
"Tough life."
"Are you making fun of me?"
"Not at all. But I do think I need to get you home."
"Really?" she asked, with an impish smile.
Damn, this was hard! He needed to divert the conversation. It would compromise him to get involved with her now.
"Do you mind if I ask you something?"
"Of course not."
"Why does this mean so much to you?"
Paula sat back to contemplate her answer. The truth was complex and she'd never told it to anyone before – not even Philippe.
"When I was growing up my father spent a good deal of time in Africa," she paused. His eyes urged her to continue.
"He was collecting artwork to establish the gallery, but he also took a ton of old-fashioned cine film on the side. He had the attic in our home converted into a kind of makeshift cinema. From the age of about three I was watching my father's documentaries on the dark continent."
"Must have been fascinating."

"It was. But despite my privileged upbringing, I never went to Africa myself."

"Why?"

"Three reasons. First, I had built Africa up to be such an incredible place in my mind, that I knew the reality could never match my dream. I didn't want to burst the bubble."

"Sounds reasonable."

"Second, I loved the animals so much, and feared them so little, I was convinced visiting Africa for the first time would be the last thing I did."

"You'd see a hungry lion, call pussycat, and become lunch."

"Exactly."

"And third?"

"Third, I decided that when I *did* Africa I wanted to *do* it a certain way. I wanted it to be me, my guide, and the animals. No other tourists around to spoil the experience. I didn't care if I broke a nail, a limb, or lost my life when I was out there. But at night I wanted to go back to four brick walls, a hot shower, and a comfortable bed."

"I see," he smiled.

She was surprised at how open and genuine his smile was. At last that icy exterior seemed to be melting.

Vernon was astonished at what he was hearing. He had hoped to bring her back to a place of sobriety where their relationship could remain firmly on a business footing – for now. He hadn't expected to uncover a deeper and more sensitive side to a woman he was already impressed by. But he was hooked now. "So what happened?" he asked.

"I found a place in Africa where I *could* do it the way I wanted. I had enough money to pay the hefty price tag. And I guess I was at a time in my life when if it was the last thing I did, it didn't matter."

"Sounds like you'd had some kind of crisis?"

"Not at all. There was nothing. I seemed to have it all, and yet I had nothing. Africa was the one thing left that I really wanted to do, so I just decided it was time. Are you really interested in all this?"

"Absolutely. Go on."

“Well, the moment I set foot on African soil I just felt like -” she paused.

“Like you’d found home?”

“Yes. Exactly. That first night out in the bush, we stopped by a waterhole. My guide told me I could get out for a drink. As I stood there under a sky like I have never seen before, a dozen rhino walked right past me to the waterhole.”

“You must have been frightened.”

“There was no room for fear. I was so full of awe, and wonder, and excitement, fear just wasn’t a part of it. You know, I swear you just don’t know how many stars there are in heaven, until you have seen the sky at night from African soil.”

He observed how she sparkled at the memories of Africa, making a mental note of that fact.

“It was as though my whole life had been a rehearsal for that moment in time. As though I’d just been missing the point up to that moment. Does this make any kind of sense?”

“It makes perfect sense,” he said genuinely.

“When I came back to Los Angeles, I felt empty. My father died a short time later and I inherited the gallery – and all the responsibility that goes with it. I became wound up in the Hollywood scene, and I guess I just became trapped.”

There was an awkward silence. She’d never opened up like this to anyone before. Philippe could never have known the old yearning, the passion he’d stirred in her on the fateful day he’d decided to take her along to Charlene’s presentation. Ever since she’d returned from Africa the one thing she really wanted to do was the one thing that eluded her. She wanted to make a difference. More than that, she wanted to be *known* for making a difference, so she could cause others to follow where she led. But any method of achieving that had always been beyond her grasp – until now.

She hadn’t liked the idea of being in charge of the fundraiser to start with – that was all Philippe’s doing. But the covert mission, that was another matter. After meeting Charlene and learning what was really at stake, she was prepared to give everything, in fact she already had, to make this mission work. She ached to achieve what no one else had managed, to be responsible for finally exposing what was really going on. And having become part of this unlikely team of collaborators, she had met the most exciting man she could ever imagine – that was icing on the cake. The fickle finger of fate was certainly a quirky and unpredictable master of her life.

"So," she said, taking a deep breath. "How are you going to get the filming done?"

"Some of it will be open. These characters are all carrying digital cameras. We've intercepted some messages being emailed to their friends back here, along with photos."

"No doubt saying they're all having a wonderful time."

"Pretty much, yes."

Paula shuddered. "And what about the stuff you can't film openly?"

"Pinhole cameras."

"You say that like it's something you do everyday."

"Not every day," he grinned.

"I see," she said trying to sound intelligent, but wondering what on earth his average day was like. Did he even have such a thing as an average day?

"You're not going to - I mean - you won't have to - will you –"

"Will I have to kill an animal not to blow my cover?"

"Will you?"

"I sincerely hope not."

Their eyes locked. Paula wasn't sure she was happy with that answer. It was all rapidly becoming deadly serious. What had she got herself in to?

She had another glass of wine and ordered a cognac. In the blur that followed, the next thing she remembered was laughing and stumbling towards her front door, with a blatantly sober Vernon following behind.

"Whoa! That wine sure catches up with you," she slurred.

"Here are your keys, Paula." He tried to place them in her hand, but she tripped into his arms.

"Whoops. Sorry." Staring up at him, Paula grabbed Vernon's face and kissed him. "That was nice," she murmured, reaching up to kiss him again.

"Paula," he said firmly.

"What's wrong?"

"Nothing, I just don't think ..."

He couldn't take his eyes off her. The longer Paula held him, the more Vernon was helpless to resist. She'd hooked him, and they both knew it. And now she was going to reel him in. Well, hell, how much was it really going to compromise him anyway?

SILHOUETTED BY THE HARSH glare of the morning light, Vernon's strong figure filled the arched frame of Paula's balcony window.

Entering the room from behind, wrapped in a white towel, Paula stopped to admire him before speaking.

"Good morning," she said softly.

"Morning," he replied, without turning around.

"I thought I'd better let you know I was coming. I wouldn't want to startle a man of your skills. A girl might end up dead."

"You were quite safe. I don't attack unarmed women. And besides, I heard you coming."

"Seemed like you were a million miles away. What were you thinking about?"

"Nothing really."

"Okay, I can take a hint."

She turned to leave, wondering how he could be so cold after the night they had just shared together. He was upon her before she saw him move, taking her hands gently but firmly to prevent her escape. His touch was welcome but his eyes gave nothing away.

"Listen," she began, trying to sound calm and in control. "In case you're concerned about what happened, don't be. It doesn't have to change our business relationship - "

"Paula..."

"Having an affair with my own personal spy, I feel like a regular Bond girl," she quipped.

"Paula..."

"Who knows how this is all going to end - "

"Paula!"

"Sorry. What?"

"I like you Paula, I like you a lot. But I think it's in both our interests to wait until after the mission before we even think about talking about this."

"Sure. I understand. That makes sense. No problem. The mission is what matters."

He took her in his arms, and she melted into his chest, wondering if she would ever see him again after she said good-bye that morning.

Chapter 4

Flying with the red sun behind it, a charter plane soared high over the vast and spectacular Zimbabwean landscape. Looking out of his small window, Vernon admired a herd of giraffe gracefully running across the endless plains below.

Zebras scattered from the primitive airfield in Bulawayo at the sound of the approaching aircraft. A stair-truck was driven out to meet the passengers, mainly starry-eyed tourists getting their taste of Africa. Vernon scanned the horizon and spotted Charlene leaning against her jeep, Shaka sitting on the hood wagging his tail expectantly. She waved.

"Vernon O'Brien?"

"I'm not that easy to spot, am I?"

"Not if I hadn't had your every feature described to me in detail by Paula." She paused. "Listen, before we go anywhere, I have a question."

"Fire away."

"I know you're a mercenary, and I know what you army types are like. For all I know, you could be one of these hunters yourself…"

"Let me stop you right there, Ms Tynsworth. I promise you I've never shot anything except a human in my life."

Charlene wasn't quite sure how to take that, but Shaka barked his approval.

"Well, I guess that's okay then," Charlene smiled.

As soon as he'd collected his luggage they climbed into the jeep. Shaka jumped onto Vernon's lap, licking him and wagging his tail.

"You really must be okay judging by that reaction," Charlene laughed. "He doesn't take to most people that way."

"He's a feisty one, what's his name?"

"Shaka."

"As in Shaka Zulu, the warrior?"

"Yes. When I found the little fella, he'd been dumped in the trash after being almost beaten to death by a local hunting club. As he survived that I thought he'd earned his name."

"How could anyone do that to you, eh Shaka?"

"Man doesn't need a reason to do evil; it's in his nature. Obviously the hunters got pissed off when Shaka didn't respond to their electric shock collar training."

Shaking his head in disgust, Vernon stroked Shaka who in turn nuzzled into the strong man's touch.

Thirty minutes later they had hit a red dirt road, Charlene asking a million questions as they went.

"I know you're staying at the hunting lodge for half of your time here, but where are you going to be staying when you're supposed to be on business?"

"I'm booked at the Harare Sheraton, but I'll need to find somewhere closer to the lodge for surveillance."

"You're quite welcome to share my campsite. I assume we'll be spending a bit of time there discussing the mission anyway. And I'm sure a man like you is used to roughing it."

"Anywhere's fine, I appreciate the offer."

"Here we are then. Home sweet home."

Vernon looked out at a huge shipping container in the middle of nowhere.

"You live in that?"

"Food and shelter are all I require, everything else is a luxury."

"But why a shipping container?"

"Too many of my other homes were either broken into or burnt to the ground. I had to outsmart the bastards somehow."

After unlocking a series of heavy-duty bolts, Charlene unlatched the container's 'door'.

"It's much safer too," she explained. "Once I'm inside nobody's getting in or out."

"How the hell did you get it out here?"

"The Red Cross foreign aid supplies are shipped over in these. And whenever their trucks pass by I have them relocate me to a new area. Keeps me one step ahead."

"You seem to have thought of everything."

"I have to, I'm all I've got out here."

Vernon studied her. She was a remarkably courageous, passionate woman. She'd elected to give up everything to fight for a cause she believed in more than life itself and to do it on her own – that was gutsy.

Paula was a passionate and courageous woman too, but at the end of the day she was still living in the luxury of Beverly Hills and Rodeo Drive, never looking death in the face, as he had done so often. She was warm and cuddly and obviously attracted to him, but he suspected the excitement of having a relationship with someone like him would be a passing fad once something else new and exciting grabbed her attention.

He admitted to himself it would be nice to have a stable companion in his life, but as attractive as Paula was he considered it was unlikely to be her. But Charlene, that was a different matter altogether. This woman was almost a female version of himself.

When night fell, Charlene set up a tarpaulin tent roof extending from each side of the container, while Vernon lit a campfire.

"Most of my so-called friends abandoned me when I left the States to work in Africa," she explained. "The rest tried to talk me out of going, thinking I'd gone mad."

"What did you tell them?"

"Let's just say I haven't received any Christmas cards since."

"Ever been married?"

"No. No time. You?"

"No. No time. It's a matter of priorities, isn't it?"

"Priorities – yes, that's it exactly."

Their eyes locked for a moment, before Charlene broke the connection to clear up the dinner dishes.

"Let me give you a hand with those."

"No need. I'm used to it. But thanks anyway."

"Well, I better hit the sack then. What are the sleeping arrangements?"

"I've set up a bed for you inside, or there's a spare hammock out here with me."

"Out here?"

"The humidity in the container can be a bit much on hot nights like this."

"What about wild animals?"

"A predator will only attack if it's threatened, injured, or protecting young. And they rarely approach a campfire."

"'Rarely'? I think I'll take my chances in the oven."

"You'll regret it."

He took one last look at the night sky sparkling in her eyes, and went to bed for an entirely sleepless night of deliberating over his options.

THE NIGHT OF THE BIG GALA fundraiser had finally arrived. Hundreds of guests mingled under a banner in Gooding's Art Gallery that read: 'AFRICARNIVAL' CHARITY GALA NIGHT; the whole place pulsating with excitement.

Given a total jungle-theme makeover, the gallery displayed African artifacts, soft big-cat toys, large leafy trees sprouting from huge pots, and fake fire torches. On a temporary stage an African band played hot, up-tempo jungle music which many of gathered throng took great pleasure in dancing to.

Waiters wore African tribal outfits. Guests were mainly dressed 'out of Africa'. Those who weren't dancing moved around the room with champagne in their hands, admiring Harbens' paintings, while others sat at their designated tables.

Ecstatic with the turn-out, Paula dazzled the room wearing a gold-shot peach chiffon dress. She spotted Joan talking graciously, as she always did, with potential donors and raised her glass in a toast across the crowd. Joan, dressed in an exquisite sequined leopard-print dress, smiled and raised her glass in reply.

Philippe was bouncing off walls in excitement, wearing a zebra-striped suit with a vivid pink bow-tie. Tom was decked out like 'Indiana Jones' and was studying one of the paintings when Paula sidled up to him from behind.

"Hey."

"Hey," he replied, spinning to face her. "It's quite a turn out."

"Yes it is. Mind if I ask you something?"

"Sure."

"It's about this Vernon O'Brien."

Philippe loomed up before Paula could get another word out. He was obviously already under the influence of several glasses of champagne and lusting after his old boyfriend, but little Paula said or did ever escaped his attention.

"What about him?" Philippe asked Paula probingly.

Paula flushed. "Oh, nothing."

Tom looked at Philippe knowingly and decided to excuse himself.

"Something you're not telling me?" Philippe asked.

"Don't be ridiculous. Our relationship is strictly professional."

"Uh huh. Who said otherwise? Next thing you'll be telling me I'm not gay. Honestly, Paula, you don't want to get tangled up with a man like that. Trust me. I know," he looked after Tom longingly. "They're never around when you want them."

"I know that," she sighed.

"You know what I think? I think you're projecting your own need to be seen as a hero onto someone you think actually is one."

Her mouth fell open. "That's very deep for you, Philippe."

"I have my deep moments. And I know you better than you think."

Entering as if she were a Spanish superstar, Lisa suddenly burst in grabbing everyone's attention.

"Arrreeebaaa!!!" she trilled.

"How disgustingly vulgar," Philippe snorted in disgust

"She's not wearing what I think she's wearing, is she?" Paula whispered.

"I'm afraid so," Philippe replied, dramatically turning his head away.

Many of the guests looked down their noses in distaste when they noticed Lisa was unbelievably wearing a long fur coat. Registering the embarrassing mistake she'd made, Lisa quickly shed the coat and dumped it on a passing waiter.

"Oh my God!" Philippe gasped.

Underneath the coat Lisa was wearing a black micro mini skirt, high heels, and an extremely tight tiger-print boob tube.

"Remind me to fire her, will you?" Paula hissed to Philippe.

"It will be my pleasure."

At that moment the band finished their set and the leader singer took the microphone to make announcements.

"Ladies and gentlemen, may I have your attention please? I'd ask you now to give a warm welcome to our special guest this evening, Hollywood legend, Joan Taylor!"

Joan glided onto the stage, accompanied by generous applause from the crowd.

"Thank you," she smiled. "But I wish they'd stop calling me that – 'legend'. I'm not dead yet!"

Everyone laughed on cue.

"A lot of people seem to be assuming that I'm the sole benefactor of this event. Well, I'd like to set the record straight on that. This wonderful evening was put together by many generous contributors."

Philippe straightened up, readying himself for praise.

"So I would like you to join with me in congratulating one woman in particular who made this fantastic evening possible."

Philippe sank back, the wind taken out of his sails.

"Would you please charge your glasses and drink a toast to Paula Gooding!"

"To Paula Gooding!" everyone echoed.

Much to Paula's surprise a spotlight hit her and the entire crowd gave her a standing ovation. Overwhelmed, tears of joy welled in her eyes. Nudging her, Philippe threw an 'I told you you'd get all the glory' look at his boss.

In the background Lisa screwed up her face in jealousy.

"Of course, Paula could not have put all of this together on her own," Joan continued. "So please raise your glasses once more to Paula's faithful and invaluable assistant, Philippe Dante!"

"To Philippe Dante!" the crowd cheered.

Philippe stood straight and took an exaggerated bow.

"Okay. Now that I have your undivided attention I would like to ask you all to open your hearts – and your wallets – as we play a special presentation."

As soon as the lights were dimmed, on a huge screen above the stage a video clip was shown of the beautiful big cats of Africa, running and playing in their natural habitat, while the African band hummed their own rendition of the immortal classic, *Born Free*. When the lights came back up there was barely a dry eye in the house.

"As many of you know," Joan fired up again. "I love these animals more than my next breath, but they are under the very real threat of extinction. So please donate generously into our collection baskets… so the animals of Africa may survive as nature intended … for these creatures are truly the brave in *The Land of the Free*."

After receiving thunderous applause, Joan left the stage and the African band performed their own version of *The Star-spangled Banner*. The parodied lyrics thanked everyone for coming, while also reminding them that they were here to help the survival of endangered big cats, ending with a chorus that made a play on the line: *Land of the Free*.

They're shot at and they're tortured,
Their pelts ferried out to sea,
But they fight bravely to survive,
In their land of the free.

Once they were convinced everyone was suitably motivated to give generously, Joan and Paula found a quiet moment to themselves.

"It's too bad Charlene couldn't be here," Paula said reflectively.

"Charlene's enjoyment will be derived from the outcome of this event, not the process."

Bursting through the crowd, Philippe excitedly interrupted them.

"Joan! Paula! I've got someone here you've just got to meet! Senator Kenneth Hay!"

Stepping out from behind Philippe, Senator Kenneth "Tex" Hay appeared in a full "Great White Hunter" outfit, except for the stereotypical Texan ten-gallon hat.

"Howdy ladies! I just had to compliment y'all, on running such a fantastic shindig!"

"Thank you, Senator," Paula gushed.

"Oh, hush now! You call me Tex. Yup, you certainly got the feel right! Matter of fact, I'm planning on visiting the Dark Continent again soon myself."

"Are you now?" Joan said very deliberately.

"Oh yes. I'm a big fan of Africa. That's why I came tonight. Can't get enough of it. Well, that and to meet you of course, Miss Taylor! I'm quite a fan of yours too! I've seen every one of your movies!"

"Is that so? Well, funnily enough, Senator, I know quite a bit about you too."

"Well I'll be," Tex beamed.

"Excuse me for butting in," Philippe interrupted. "But I thought you'd like to know that the Senator here has offered to make a donation to our Wildlife Fund." Philippe almost threw his arms around Tex in excitement, screeching to a halt only when the Senator drowned him in a disapproving scowl.

"Has he now?" Joan again spoke very slowly.

"I certainly have! I'm prepared right here, right now to sign you over a check for one million dollars!"

"Oh my God!" Paula and Philippe said as one, Philippe staggering in a near faint.

"On the proviso, of course," the Senator added, "that my good name features right next to wherever your fine charity is displayed or advertised."

"I see," Joan said, her eyes narrowing.

"I think it's about time I added the title of philanthropist to my public profile, don't you? Hell, it won't harm my political career either!"

"That's very noble of you, Senator. But a million - is that all?" Joan asked.

Paula and Philippe turned to Joan with their mouths open agog!

Tex belly-laughed. "Still the entertainer, huh?"

"Not at all," Joan said evenly. "I'm deadly serious."

"What?" Paula gasped.

“A million dollars is nothing to this Southern – gentleman. Only last year he donated a *hundred* million to the Smithsonian Institute just so he could bring in a trophy of one of the most endangered species on the planet - under the guise of research, of course.”

Suddenly everyone was stunned into silence.

“Now if only one animal you shot, stuffed and displayed is worth a hundred million to you, how much more do you think it’s worth to have your name respected next to ours?” Joan asked challengingly.

Tex studied the movie star for a moment. “Whoowee! You sure drive a hard bargain, ma'am! Hell, I may have to fire all my lawyers and hire you to do my business negotiations from now on! Okey-dokey, how much is this gonna sting me?” He pulled out his checkbook and pen, waiting for a figure.

“Absolutely nothing,” Joan replied.

“Excuse me?” the Senator asked, stunned.

“I wouldn’t let a man like you bathe in my animals’ excrements,” Joan replied, standing to face him.

Everyone in earshot gasped.

“What?” he bumbled.

“You heard me.”

“Joan?!” Paula pleaded.

“You must be the stupidest damn bitch I ever met,” Tex growled. “Here I am offering you the answer to all your prayers and you spit in my face!”

Joan ignored his taunts, signaling to two African-American doormen that they should join her.

“Do you have any idea who you’re dealing with?” the Senator blustered angrily.

“The only deal we are going to make here is whether you leave this event peacefully, or I have you thrown out,” Joan announced.

Standing menacingly behind Tex, the two doormen dressed as Zulu warriors, waited for Joan’s command.

“Are you out of your mind?” Tex yelled.

“Gentlemen,” Joan said calmly to the doormen. “Would you escort this gate-crasher out? He seems to have outstayed his welcome.”

"Yes, ma'am," said the first doorman.

"Come with us would you, sir?" asked the second.

"What? Get your goddamn nigger hands off me!"

As soon as Tex's racist remark left his lips, the doormen appeared to take great delight in grabbing him by the arms and dragging him out, causing a huge spectacle.

"You ain't heard the last from me!" Tex bellowed. "Mark my words! I ain't the kind of guy you want to mess with! Hell, I could buy Africa if I wanted!"

"I can't believe you just did that," Paula wheezed, feeling dizzy. "I thought Charlene said she didn't care where the money came from."

"She doesn't, and I suppose neither should I. But I'm sorry; I refuse to accept any amount of blood money to help him cleanse his soul."

Tossed out onto the sidewalk like a common drunk, Tex furiously struggled to his feet, only to be met with his crushed ten-gallon hat hitting him in the face. His driver raced to his aid.

"Are you alright, Senator?"

"Get the hell off me," he barked back ungratefully, turning his attention to the doormen. "I'd watch my black asses if I were you! Where I come from we still lynch your kind."

One of the doormen feigned a king hit at Tex, scaring him into his stretch limo, which screeched off as soon as he was inside.

The doormen simply smiled at each other, while inside another bottle of champagne popped. Paula was dancing with Tom, Joan chatted and laughed with Philippe, and Lisa Mendoza had expertly cornered Harbens. The artist fidgeted from one foot to the other, gazing deadpan into Lisa's seductive face until he broke away, heading straight towards Paula.

"Harbens, you dear, dear man," Paula gushed, stopping her dance to embrace the number one benefactor of the evening. "Here he is everyone, the man of the moment! There aren't too many artists who can boast they sold all their paintings at their first exhibition. Congratulations, Harbens! And thank you."

With that she tried to plant a big kiss on him but he pulled away.

"Yes, well, that's what I need to talk to you about," Harbens started uncertainly. "Could I please have a word with you in private, Ms Gooding?"

Paula looked at Harbens, her brow furrowing in confusion. "Yes, of course."

Sensing Harbens meant *now*, Tom moved away to join Joan and Philippe, while keeping a close eye on the artist.

"What now?" Philippe asked his ex.

"Who knows?" Tom shrugged.

Paula led Harbens to a quiet corner to continue the conversation. "What up?"

"I think I may have been a bit hasty."

"In what?"

"In offering as much as fifty percent of my sales to your cause."

"I beg your pardon?"

"Your charity stands to make a lot of money from my work and…"

"And so do you," she snapped back firmly.

"Yes, but I've just realized I forgot to take into account all my expenses."

Seeing where this was going, Paula braced herself. "Go on."

"Over the years I've been forced to borrow money from all sorts of people to get my career off the ground, you know for oils, brushes, canvasses. With only fifty percent coming to me, I doubt I'll even be able to recoup enough to cover my debts."

"So what are you trying to say, you want to renege on the deal?"

"No, not completely."

"Then what?"

"I was thinking more along the lines of … ten percent?"

Paula just glared at him for endless seconds.

"Alright," she finally said evenly.

"You accept?"

"Of course. I'll even introduce you personally to all the animal lovers who bought your work tonight and inform them that not as much of their hard-earned cash is going where they thought it was. I'm sure that will give your new career an interesting start."

Their eyes locked in silent adversarial confrontation.

"On second thoughts," he stammered. "This is all about helping the animals, isn't it?"

"I'm glad you see it that way," she smiled, enjoying watching him squirm.

Taking his cue to leave, Harbens got up and headed for the door, stopping for only a moment at the main entrance where Lisa boldly pushed her body against his.

Noticing Paula had finished her chat, Tom returned to her side. "What was that all about?"

"Oh nothing," she cheered. "Well, hopefully we've made enough to cover your friend's fees and pay back my overdraft. Do you think he'll be away long?"

"Vernon? Hard to say. These guys usually go to comms blackout when they're on a job. He'll contact us when he's ready."

"I hope he's okay."

"Why wouldn't he be?" Tom asked, with the merest hint of a smirk.

"You give yourself away, darling," Philippe slurred, joining them. "Are you planning to see him again?"

"I don't know," she sighed.

"Oh well, I still think you're making a mistake, but you know what they say: if you love something set it free. If it comes back it's yours. If not, it never was."

"That doesn't exactly inspire me with confidence."

"Snap out of it, would you? The night is still young and I have not yet begun to party!" Grabbing her hands, Philippe dragged Paula back onto the dance floor, winking lustfully at Tom.

Chapter 5

Vernon stepped out of Charlene's container home, sweating profusely. As she looked at the bedraggled soggy sight that had been a smooth macho man only the night before, she couldn't help but giggle.

"Told you so."

"Nothing forty-four gallons of water won't fix," he quipped.

"You ready for this?"

"Walk in the park. We at "Pest Control" are always ready."

""Pest Control"?"

"A nickname my group has been given."

"Pest Control – I love it," she smiled.

"I just have to get a few supplies, and establish my cover in Harare. Then I'll link up with the hunters some time tomorrow."

Sure enough, twenty-four hours later, Vernon was driving under the ivory tusk gates of Matupula Hunting Lodge in a hired jeep. As was customary, Laurie met his new client at the outdoor bar.

"Vincent Nash, I presume?"

"That's right. Pleased to meet you," Vernon offered Laurie his hand.

"Laurie Watson, at your service."

Two native workers grabbed Vernon's luggage.

"Bungalow twelve," Laurie ordered in their native tongue. "And get a move on!" His steely gaze watched the servants scuttle away before he returned his attention to Vernon. "Follow me, Mr. Nash, I'll show you around. You said on the phone you're mixing business and pleasure on this trip?"

"That's right. I'm working for a multinational telecommunications company."

"Really, which one?"

"I've been temporarily contracted to Bell South's African division. It seems the local elephants keep pulling up the phone lines. It's costing the company hundreds of thousands in repairs. I'm here to implement new strategies to stop them."

"A bullet through the elephants' skulls sounds like the smart and simple strategy to me."

"I agree, but the company would prefer a more politically correct solution."

"Bullshit. If I showed them how much cash they'd save doing it my way, they'd soon change their Greeny attitude," he scoffed, leading Vernon to an area designed like the "OK Corral".

Touching down in the middle of the courtyard, a scenic tours helicopter whirred noisily to the landing pad. Bending to avoid the rotor blades, Tex stepped out.

"This is an unexpected visit. What's up, Senator?" Laurie asked.

"Let's just say I got a major itch up my ass that needs scratchin'," Tex scowled. "So gimmee your best team and as much ammo as we can carry! 'Coz I'm gonna blast the crap out of as many big cats as I can lay my hands on!"

"Not a problem, Senator."

"Come on now! We ain't in the White House. Call me Tex!"

"Whatever you say - Tex. Oh, allow me to introduce you to one of your countrymen, Vincent Nash."

"Howdy partner!"

"Pleased to meet you," Vernon replied formally.

Leading the way, Laurie guided them both to the back of the lodge where the shooting range was located. Every brutal weapon known to man was on display in an open storeroom. A group of overweight and generally inept hunters were shooting at targets, instructed by an "Ivan Drago"-looking mercenary called Lertz. In contrast to the hunters, Lertz demonstrated exceptional deadly prowess.

Helping a hunter reload, another of Laurie's hired guns, Daniels, greeted the boss with a cheeky smile.

"I think you'll find all my staff skilled in making sure you get the most out of your hunts," Laurie told Vernon. "Daniels here was a member of Her Majesty's Secret Service – that is until they discovered he had links to the IRA."

"Top of the morning to ya," Daniels beamed.

"Sully there was a Green Beret."

Terry "Sully" Sullivan, a huge man with a permanent frown etched in his face, tipped his hat. "How's it going?"

"Though frankly I don't know how the fat fuck got that far," Laurie whispered loudly to Vernon.

"Piss off Laurie," Sully rumbled.

"And you?" Vernon asked.

"I was in the British SAS, until I got DD'd for being too damn good at what they taught me."

Enjoying the in-joke, Laurie's men all laughed.

"What about yourself?" Tex asked Vernon.

"I did the weekend warrior bit for three years in the army reserve, but I never saw any action."

"I reckon you could handle yourself, though. It's in your eyes," Laurie observed.

Ignoring the comment and intrigued by Lertz, Vernon asked, "Who's that?"

"That's my taxidermy man and right hand, Lertz. They say he actually escaped the French Foreign Legion."

"He don't talk much, though. Do ya, Lertz?" Daniels teased.

Lertz gave Vernon a suspicious glance, as Laurie handed his newest client a rifle.

"Here, have a shot."

Taking the rifle, Vernon lined up his shot, instinctively hitting the furthest target dead on its bulls-eye, stunning everyone.

"Shit!" Sully spluttered.

"That's some shooting," Laurie agreed.

Brushing it off, Vernon reloaded. "You don't think I meant to do that, do you?"

"That's some beginner's luck then," Daniels commented.

Vernon quickly took another few shots, purposely missing his targets by just enough, while ignoring Lertz's skeptical grimace.

"I didn't fly all this way just to shoot targets," Tex suddenly complained, getting bored. "Let's get out there."

"Alright, alright, straight after I show Vincent some of our recent kills."

Situated behind the ammo shed, Laurie proudly took Vernon to where piles of dead big game had been unceremoniously dumped. Vernon's eyes started to water, he had to quickly covered his nose, thinking he might choke from the stench. In stark contrast, Tex took in a huge gulp of air.

"Hey now, that's what I call a sweet smell."

"Sorry 'bout the smell," Laurie offered. "But we don't have anywhere else to put 'em until Lertz does his stuffing and polishing."

Completely invisible to the untrained eye, Vernon's pinhole camera flashed from his jacket on the gruesome injuries inflicted by barbed arrows that were still the animals' flesh - obviously not where the strike would have been fatal. He couldn't help wondering what kind of God in Heaven could have permitted the creation and continued existence of men who were capable of inflicting such pain on innocent animals, never mind actually taking some form of twisted, nauseating pleasure out of it. Nonetheless, the consummate professional that he was, Vernon managed to look impressed and kept up the act until he gratefully returned to humble edifice that Charlene called home.

As soon as he stepped out of his jeep, Shaka came running to Vernon's side.

"Hey there, little fella." He whisked the little Jack Russell high above his head, delighted to see at least one animal was alive and well and happy.

Shaka barked and wagged his tail, his tongue trying desperately to reach Vernon's nose for a welcome home lick.

"So, how was it?" Charlene asked.

"Do you really want to know?"

"No not really, but tell me anyway."

"I don't think he suspects anything, but he does seem to be playing it safe on the hunts. Maybe he's checking me out first."

"How many defenseless creatures did they slaughter today?"

"Too many."

"One is too many. Fucking evil pricks!"

Embarrassed by her outburst, Charlene tried to calm down. "I'm sorry. It's just all a bit much sometimes."

"I understand," he said softly, lowering Shaka to the ground. "Sometimes I think the toilet bowel of humanity needs a really good flush!"

She looked at him curiously. He was a soldier a fortune, a mercenary, a trained killer, and yet Shaka adored him and he really seemed to care about things. He was one big walking enigma.

"What about you?" she asked tentatively. "Did you have to shoot anything?"

"No, not yet. But if I keep missing them like I am, it could blow my cover."

"Well, let's just hope you can get enough evidence before that happens."

"I know something's going down in a few days at Matopo Hills, but they haven't invited me."

"Oh no, we're trying to protect the lion population there."

"This might sound cold, but catching them breaking the law, and not just bending it, is what I've been hired to do."

Charlene scowled. "I'll draw you a map in the morning, 'coz I guarantee you they're not going there for the sight-seeing. If only we had the money to hire an anti-poaching patrol," she added wistfully to herself.

A full moon glistened in the star-studded African sky as the sound of elephants munching on trees and the distant roaring of lions filled the air. She settled down in her hammock and before she knew it, fell into a stressful and exhausted sleep. Vernon pulled a blanket over her and headed inside. Shaka looked back and forth, uncertain whom he most wanted to spend the night with, finally opting to settle half way between the two.

When dawn broke the following day, the sun rose quickly over another spectacular morning, sweeping its life-giving warmth and light over the majestic land called Africa. Charlene was already up and dressed, gazing at Mother Nature's palette of startling colors in the far-off horizon.

"Good morning," a voice greeted her from behind.

"Yes it is."

"What are you doing out here so early?"

"I often stand in awe of Mother Africa. Despite all the horror, She still manages to dazzle me with Her magnificence. It's why I came. It's why I'll never leave. Africa gets into your soul."

Vernon looked at the sunrise and a herd of wildebeest on the plains ahead. "I see what you mean," he murmured, gazing at her with profound understanding and admiration.

Back in his bungalow, Vernon quietly viewed the footage he'd obtained so far. Throughout a week of hunts he'd managed to film a leopard shot in a tree, dog teams chasing a caracal over a rock-face cliff, and a black panther in a canned hunt. He observed with more than a degree of distaste, the one constant in every image was hunters' excited laughter in the background.

RELAXING ON A POOL-SIDE sun-bed in Maui, with a colorful drink by her side, Paula answered the ring of her cell phone.

"Hello?"

"Paula! Thank goodness you're alright! Where the hell are you?" Philippe asked in a highly agitated tone.

"Calm down Philippe. I'm in Maui, remember?"

"You weren't supposed to be there for another week!"

"I know, but after all the stress of organizing the Gala Night, I decided to bring it forward. Why? What's the drama?"

"The gallery's been robbed!"

Paula sat bolt upright, spilling her drink. "What? When?"

"Last night!"

"Oh my God? What did they take?"

"Everything."

"Everything? What do you mean everything?"

"Everything! The paintings! The Africarnival Gala funds from the safe! Everything! The bastards even stole our filing cabinets!"

"Oh no," she groaned, sinking back into her sun bed.

"And that's not the worst part! Somehow, none of our security cameras or alarms were armed, so our insurance company is refusing to come to the party!"

"Have you called the police?"

"Of course. They're on their way. Oh Paula, what are we going to do?"

"I don't know - panic!"

"I'm doing that already!"

"Alright, Philippe. I'm taking the first plane home. I'll call you the minute I arrive at LAX, okay?"

"Okay."

She pressed the end button, trying hard not to cry.

WHILE ALL THOSE around him sank into a pleasant level of inebriation, Vernon remained a picture of sobriety. With a dozen hunters, six rangers and another dozen native staff running around, the small outdoor bar in Matupula was full to overflowing.

"Yeehaa! What a day," Tex shouted. "The next round's on me!"

Hunters and staff alike cheered their approval.

"Hey Senator – I mean, Tex - you never did tell me what you were so grouchy about when you arrived," Laurie commented.

"Don't ask!"

"Woman trouble?"

"Why would you say that?" Tex raised his eyebrows.

"Only a woman could provoke that reaction. Ever had woman trouble, Vinny?"

"You might say that," Vernon joined the conversation.

"Ah, women - God's perverse little joke on mankind," Laurie mused. "Hey, Vincent, come out the back with us, I wanna show you something."

Tex grinned broadly, knowing full well what the Lodge owner had in mind.

Crammed into a shed full of animal carcasses, Vernon followed Laurie, Sully and Tex to a huge tarpaulin-covered box.

Covering his nose and mouth against the stench, he secretly switched on his pinhole camera.

"Thanks guys, but this is an experience you could have spared me."

"This isn't it, ya wally," Sully scoffed. "That is!"

"What is?"

"Well, pull back the cloth and take a look," Laurie suggested.

Doing as Laurie asked, Vernon was suddenly confronted by a full-grown male lion pouncing with its full force hard against a cage wall.

"Shit!"

Laurie, Tex, and Sully all doubled over laughing.

"Vincent Nash, say hello to Arnie," Laurie finally said, when he could catch his breath again.

"I still get a kick out of seeing you do that to the initiates," Tex spluttered.

Sully bashed at the lion with a club to enhance the performance. "We call him Arnie 'coz he's like the "Terminator". No matter what we do to him he just keeps coming back for more."

"You gotta admire him though," said Laurie. "Even when I put a bullet in his skull, it just lodged there and the tough bastard is still here today!"

Vernon was unable to take his eyes of the battle-scarred and brutalized lion.

"You'll have to forgive his temper,' Sully added. "He's that hungry that if he had room in there he'd probably chew off his own limbs!"

"I'm sure if we really tried we could finish him off, but I'm kinda curious to see how long he'll last, and besides I've got one final job for him," Laurie revealed, winking at Sully.

If it wasn't that his professional training kept his emotions in check, Vernon might have spun three times surfacing at the doorway to find all three of them with their necks snapped like twigs.

STEPPING OUT into the arrivals lounge at LAX, still reeling from the news of the art gallery break-in, Paula barely reacted when two plain-clothed detectives approached her.

"Paula Gooding?"

"Yes."

"My name is Detective Dan Jones and this is my partner, Detective Steven Bracken."

They folded out their ID badges.

"LAPD," Jones explained.

"LAPD? Gee, you boys don't mess around. Have you caught whoever broke into my gallery already?"

"Ah, no ma'am. We're actually here to take you down to the station for questioning on a completely different matter."

"What?"

"If you'd come with us, Miss."

Dazed and confused, she followed the detectives, wondering if she'd just walked through the Looking-Glass.

A reporter in the background spotted Paula as she was escorted out. "There she is!"

Flooding around her before the detectives had a chance to explain, Paula found herself surrounded by reporters and cameramen.

"Miss Gooding? Is it true you have been using your art gallery as a front to misappropriate charity funds for your own personal use?"

"What? Of course not! How ridiculous!"

"Then how do you explain the fact that you've just returned from a five-star resort in Maui, straight after running a fundraiser?"

"One thing has absolutely nothing to do with the other!"

"Not according to an employee of yours. A Lisa Mendoza. She claims your extravagant lifestyle is totally sustained by you running phony charity events."

"Well, that's obviously a lie. Africarnival was the first and only charity event I've ever been involved in."

"Alright then, tell us, where has all the money raised from your Africarnival been distributed to?"

Jesus, she thought. She couldn't answer that question even if her gallery hadn't been robbed. She couldn't reveal the covert mission to the media – not yet anyway. And now the gallery *had* been robbed, she saw their point. It didn't look good. "No comment," she said, in shock.

With the press jumping on her like a hungry pack of hyenas, Paula turned to the two detectives who helped escort her away.

Philippe was positively in a tailspin. He shot at least two red lights on his way to collect Paula from the police station, muttering all the way that he'd never liked Lisa in the first place. But why on earth would she accuse Paula of this crime? It didn't make sense. Or did it? Her preoccupation with being a star; that was it! She'd get her fifteen minutes of fame and try to capitalize on it to the max, maybe even get a movie made of how she exposed Paula. Oh God, it was horrible. He ran another red light.

Paula looked disheveled. There was a vacant expression in her eyes that disturbed Philippe greatly.

"Darling, what have they done to you?"

"Nothing. I'm fine, Philippe. Really."

Suddenly Philippe threw his arms around her and Paula dissolved into a pile of tears on his shoulder.

"There, there, sweetheart. Don't you worry about anything. We'll sort this all out. You'll see."

Carrying her luggage, Philippe guided Paula to his sports car where she sat solemnly in the passenger seat.

"I don't believe it. Until a full FBI and IRS investigation has been carried out, all my assets are being frozen! How am I ever going to explain to Vernon where his money is?"

"I'm sure he'll understand." There was a long silence before Philippe added, "I spoke to Joan. Apparently, none of the media had the guts to accuse her of foul play, but at the same time they're refusing to acknowledge any of her claims about your innocence."

"That figures. Never let the facts get in the way of a good story."

"Yes, well that story hasn't exactly been that good for us. We're receiving quite a few angry messages from the charity night donors, either demanding a refund or saying they'll be canceling their checks because of the scandal. So even if we find the missing funds we're still screwed."

"Any more good news?"

"Ah, Lisa phoned in her resignation and Harbens is threatening to sue."

"Sue? Sue for what?"

"Misrepresentation."

"How can he? We had a written agreement. I kept it in my diary. Oh no …"

"That's right, the diary from your desk – that's gone too."

"I knew she was up to something," Lisa said smarmily to the media, relishing the limelight. She casually tossed her hair over her shoulder, noticing with a glance how good she looked in the reflection of Gooding's Art Gallery's exterior window. "But I couldn't quite put my finger on it. She's very cunning. On the surface, she pretends to be this generous benevolent charity queen. But at the same time she spends all her money on expensive exuberant luxuries."

Later that night in Paula's apartment, Philippe cradled his friend in his arms as Lisa's exposé aired on primetime television. Continuing her well-orchestrated litany of lies, Lisa proudly told all to the nation.

"I bet the only reason she hired a less-than-fortunate ethnic girl like me was so she could look good in front of her friends! Or perhaps she planned to pin her crime on me while she was conveniently out of town. Oh yes, she's one scheming, scamming loco bitch!"

Jumping into crisis mode, Philippe got up heading for the kitchen. "I'll get the champagne," he announced.

"Champagne? How can you think of having champagne at a time like this?"

"Darling, there's no bad time for champagne. Besides, this is cause for a celebration."

"How do you figure that?"

"Well, this is definitely the worst thing she could have done to you, so it's all plain sailing from here."

"You know what," she grinned. "I do believe you're right. Pop the champagne."

"Your wish is, oh it was my wish actually - whatever."

A moment later a loud POP was followed by the swooshing sound of bubbles filling crystal.

Chapter 6

Following the crack of gunshots in Matopo Hills there was muffled laughter and cheering. Wind rustled through the long grass on the ridge peek of a hill. Suddenly a patch moved forward, and Vernon peered out, decked in earth-colored camouflage gear. His telephoto lens focused down in the valley where the hunters and their dogs were brutalizing a pride of lions.

Disgusted, Vernon slid out his sniper rifle for a closer look. Aiming at the hunters, he froze when he heard some dry twigs crack behind him. Turning only his eyes, he discovered to his horror another pride of lions was curious about the scuffle below. Seemingly uninterested in him, the lions settled nearby to watch the drama play out.

After the hunters took their glory photos, they loaded the lion carcasses into the back of their jeeps and prepared to head home. Between a rock and a hard place, Vernon remained motionless, hoping *his* lions would lose interest and depart. Barely breathing, he was thankfully attracting no unwanted attention from either the predators by his side, nor the predators down below - until a black mamba snake slithered towards him. Every sense was alert, his eyes darting between the snake, the lions and the hunters.

He prayed, something he rarely did, that the snake wouldn't spook the lions, nor slither too close to his position. Either event might give him away. Naturally this was not to be. As the snake sensed mainly by movement, and Vernon wasn't making any, it crept its way stealthily towards him, totally unaware of the fatal mistake it was making. Before the snake saw him move, Vernon expertly and silently killed it with a single blow from the butt of his riffle. Unfortunately, this caused the nearby lions to react.

The alpha lioness glared at him, padding her paw threateningly on the undergrowth. She indicated, with a flick of her head to the left and the right, that the rest of the pride should back off, taking the cubs to safety. Reluctantly they obeyed her, lionesses carrying their infants away in their mouths.

Much as his self-preservation instincts were telling him to kill the lions and get the hell out of there, he heard Charlene's voice over and over in his head. "A predator will only attack if it's threatened, injured or protecting young."

"Nice pussycat," he whispered. "I won't hurt you, if you don't hurt me. We got a deal?"

The lioness snorted disapprovingly and backed away. Vernon let out the breath he was unaware he was holding, not believing what had just happened. He rolled, relieved, onto his back, accidentally knocking his camera with his elbow. It loudly began to rewind. The unfamiliar noise startled the retreating lioness, who roared in response.

"Look! Up there! More lions!" Sully shouted.

Rapid gunfire filled the air, frightening every animal in the area.

"Cease fire! Cease fire!" Laurie yelled. "Stupid pricks," he muttered to himself, adding a brief explanation – "They're gone!"

"Well, what are we waiting for? Let's go get 'em!" Tex bellowed.

"There's not enough daylight left," reasoned Sully.

"So?"

"So," Laurie explained, "man may rule the daylight hours, but the night definitely belongs to the wild."

"Humph!" the Texan growled.

"Pack up your things, boys! Time to go home!"

Doing as Laurie commanded, everyone prepared to leave, except Lertz whose steely eyes hadn't stopped scanning the horizon. He lifted his sniper rifle for a closer look.

Vernon raised his own rifle to check what was happening below. For a heartbeat it seemed Vernon and Lertz had each other in their sights. Vernon slowly squeezed his trigger.

"Come on, Lertz," Laurie ordered. "Its nothing!"

Holding his aim for a moment longer, Lertz gradually lowered his rifle.

Vernon bowed his head in relief. He couldn't have lived with himself if he'd been through all this, got all this evidence, and blown his cover at the eleventh hour.

Night had fallen by the time Vernon returned to Charlene's campsite. A fire was already crackling outside her container home. In the distance a kudu called in alarm, alerting others in its herd that hunting lion were near. Vervet monkeys scuttled in trees overhead, not yet having settled in for night's wary sleep. Charlene sat gazing at the fire, wistfully seeing images in the flames of a time when all creatures on earth could live in dignity and freedom.

Vernon looked at her without speaking. The first thing he did was head straight for her canteen to douse himself with water, as if to somehow spiritually clean away the horror and carnage he'd witnessed that day. Shaka looked at him, his head cocked on one side in curiosity. Charlene had no such doubts in her mind.

"Was it that bad?" she asked rhetorically.

"If I live to be a thousand, I'll never understand it," he replied simply.

She pulled out a flask of whisky she kept for medicinal purposes and poured it into two tin cups.

"Here," she offered.

"Thanks," he said quietly, taking the drink and sitting by her side.

Shaka promptly curled up by their feet, happy his "pack" was together again.

"I'm beginning to understand your fascination with these animals," Vernon said suddenly, gazing into the fire.

"Oh?"

"I had what you might call a life-changing experience today."

She said nothing, her eyes urging him to continue.

"Before I met you I wouldn't have thought twice about killing, rather than being killed. But your words kept ringing in my head, and I took a chance that went against everything I've ever been trained to do."

She smiled both with satisfaction and joy in the knowledge that another human was beginning to understand these animals the way she did. She continued to listen as Vernon told her about his encounter with the pride above the valley on Matopo Hills.

"I just can't believe I didn't become lunch," he finally concluded.

"Lions, unlike man, are not opportunistic predators."

"You know … I could seriously consider moving over here."

"Yeah, right," she scoffed. "Once you get your money in your hot little hand you'll be off to the next "Pest Control" mission."

"A man can change, you know. Maybe I'll buy a ranch out here and head up your anti-poaching patrol."

"Those lions really got to you, didn't they? Next thing you'll be telling me is you don't mind sleeping outside."

"After today, anything's possible!"

With that he rushed inside to get his bed, Shaka hot on his heels, barking. Charlene giggled to herself, and was still giggling when Vernon returned to put his blanket and pillow into the spare hammock next to hers.

"There." He admired his handiwork. "Perfect."

He hopped in, settling easily, having been used to sleeping in much worse. Shaka instantly jumped on top of him and licked his nose.

"Hey, I don't need a bath. Well, that's not strictly true, but cool it, will ya?" He turned to Charlene, then looked at the campfire. "Animals are afraid of the fire, right?"

"Sure," she smiled, getting into her own hammock. "About as much as you are." With that she rolled away from him, silently grinning to herself.

The following morning he thought it was about time he checked in with Paula. Using a satellite phone Vernon rang the gallery, half hoping Philippe would answer and Paula would be out shopping somewhere. Although he assured himself he had no reason to feel guilty about anything, after all he'd made no commitment to Paula, save for the mission, and in any event, nothing had happened with Charlene, yet he still felt he'd betrayed her affection. Why did everything always have to be so damn complicated? Come on, he thought, pick up – Philippe. No such luck. Paula answered and instantly poured her heart out about the recent robbery and subsequent vilification she'd received on national prime-time media.

"Oh, Vernon," she sobbed. "I don't know what to do. If I tell them where I planned to distribute the money, I'll have to reveal the mission, but if I don't I'm facing jail."

"Then tell them the truth."

"What? How can I? Won't that blow your cover?"

"Not if you can hold them off for a few more days."

"I can try," she said, trying to sound brave. "Okay. I will. No problem. A few days. I can do that. I miss you."

There were long seconds of silence as Vernon glanced towards Charlene who was playing with Shaka in the distance.

"Whoops," Paula quickly added. "Did I say that out aloud? Sorry. It's been a stressful week."

"Listen, I have to go, I'll call you back in a day or so. Hang in there, kid."

Paula heard the line go dead.

"Kid?" she spat to herself. "Well, goodbye to you too."

"Trouble in paradise?" Philippe jibed from behind her.

"Don't you say it."

"Say what?"

"I told you so."

"Would I?"

"Oh yes."

"Come on, darling, we have more important things to worry about."

Being reminded of that fact didn't help her mood – it didn't help it one bit.

WITH HIS MISSION all but accomplished, Vernon could have packed up and left Zimbabwe at any time. But there were a few loose ends he still wanted to tie up. He wanted some more background on Laurie's hired thugs. He wanted to know the full story behind Arnie, the lion. And if he was to be honest with himself, he wanted a few more days to see if there was any chance of becoming a more permanent feature in Charlene's life.

He returned to Matupula right after his call with Paula, and found Tex and Laurie already geared up for a fresh hunt. He readily accepted the offer to join them, not expecting he would be invited to take part in a kill – Tex was far to keen for the kill shot to let anyone else have that privilege, so he thought. For the second time that morning, he was wrong. Tex said it wasn't fair that Vernon hadn't had the thrill of his own kill yet, when he himself had had so many. This time there was no wriggling out of it.

Both Laurie and Tex held their breath as Vernon aimed at a large leopard the scent hounds had tracked down. Slowly he lined up the big male in his sights, squeezed the trigger on his rifle, fired, and missed the animal by inches, sending it escaping off into the bush.

"Shit," he shouted, trying to sound angry.

"Hell, even I could of hit that," Tex bellowed.

"What's on your mind, Vinny?" Laurie asked cautiously.

"What do you mean?"

"You had him in your sights. Your posture was strong. You'd have to be day-dreaming to miss a shot like that."

"I do have a lot on my plate at the moment… you know… with work."

"I think it's a bit more than that," Laurie said suspiciously.

"Come on, Vinny. We're all men here. Spit it out," Tex urged.

Thinking on his feet, Vernon responded truthfully. "Ever been in love with two women?"

"Women! Why is it always women?!" Laurie scowled.

"What's the matter, Lawrence? Ain't you never been in love?" Tex laughed. "Take my advice, boy, love 'em both!"

Suddenly a few drops of rain rapidly turned into a downpour.

"Oh well, that puts an end to today's hunting," Laurie announced.

"Goddamn it! We only just started," Senator Hay complained. "Come on, one more – "

Stepping forward to try and encourage Laurie to allow them to stay just a little longer, Tex lost his footing and fell squarely on his backside in mud. Laurie and Vernon both helped him up as the deluge developed into sheets of solid water, reducing visibility to zero. It continued that way, unrelentingly into the night, not slackening off until dawn broke the following day.

CHARLENE STOOD in her doorway as the sun rose, creating a startling rainbow across the landscape. Suddenly she began to cry.

Thank God for the start of the rainy season, she said to herself. In a few weeks the animals would be safe for a while, without the worry of being blown apart by some hunter.

As if hearing her private thoughts, Vernon stepped up from inside her container home to join her.

"Are you alright?"

"What? Of course. I'm fine."

"That's not rain on your cheek."

"Sometimes I just cry, you know?"

"No, I don't."

"I cry for Africa. I cry for its animals. I cry for this whole fucked-up world! I just cry, okay?"

This wasn't winning him any points. Understandably, Charlene wasn't about to open up or trust anyone. She'd learned to fend for herself, and she had no love of human beings in general. Yet she had so much to offer, if only there was some way to creak open the door.

"This whole fucked-up world?" he shouted back at her. "This whole fucked-up world! What's wrong with it?" Stepping out into the rain, Vernon was instantly saturated. "It ain't all that fucked up, is it? Look!" Jumping in the biggest puddle he could find, he splashed around like a big kid.

Totally surprised, and seeing Vernon in an entirely different light, as hard as she tried Charlene couldn't hold back her laughter.

"What are you laughing at? I thought you said everything was fucked up."

"You're an idiot!"

"Am I?"

"Yes!"

Stepping forward, Vernon challenged her. "Well, you're full of compliments as usual."

"And I'm quite happy to stay dry too, so back off, soggy boy!"

"You know what? I've had enough of your lip! Come here!"

"What? No!"

Before she could stop him, Vernon grabbed her around the waist and threw her over his shoulder. Kicking and screaming all the way, Charlene had no chance against Vernon's determination. He held her like that until she was saturated before doing the unthinkable: dumping her into a huge dirty puddle.

"Oh! You prick! You're dead!"

Jumping to her feet, Charlene scooped up a handful of slimy mud and tossed it at Vernon.

Looking down at the huge mud stain on his shirt, Vernon scooped up his own mud pie.

"If it's a war you want, it's a war you'll get!"

Pitching his mud like a baseball, it hit Charlene in the face.

"You're a real gentleman, aren't you?"

"Start acting like a lady and I might treat you like one!"

Returning fire, Charlene hit him in the back of the head as he tried to duck.

"Sorry pal! No ladies here!"

Following through with a second throw, Charlene hit Vernon in the head again.

"I can see that," he agreed.

Deflecting one of her throws, Vernon caught her at the wrist.

"Hey! That's cheating!" Charlene buckled over and with her free hand retaliated by scooping up more mud and shoving it down Vernon's pants. "You picked the wrong girl to mess with!"

Pushing another handful into Vernon's unsuspecting face, Charlene temporarily blinded him, giving herself enough time to attack again. Sensing her charge, Vernon managed to catch both her arms, avoiding the muddy assault.

Wrestling upright, Charlene was no match for Vernon's strength, but while he was laughing she took the advantage and sweep-tripped his leg so hard that he was tackled to the ground. Straddling her opponent, Charlene yelled with a victory cry.

"Wanna play rough, huh?"

Turning the tables, Vernon flipped Charlene up and over the top of him and pinned her down. Infuriated she struggled against his strength.

"Give up," he ordered.

"Never!"

Lifting her knee, Charlene hit Vernon in the balls, winding him. Quickly, she rolled over on top again while he was still suffering.

"That's it! No more Mr. Nice Guy!"

Kicking into assassin mode, Vernon quickly wrestle-maneuvered around in the mud, re-pinning Charlene down, this time giving her no chance of escape. Caught in a tangled mess of arms and legs, the pair found that their wet bodies were firmly pushed together.

"That's not fair! Let me go!"

"No! I'm quite comfortable, thank you very much!"

"Alright! Alright! I give up! That's what you wanted to hear, isn't it? You're a real man! You win!"

"Sorry, not good enough."

"What?"

"I've done everything you wanted, and more. So how about you drop the man-hating feminist act and try being nice for a change?"

"Alright! For crying out loud! Just let me go!"

Relaxing his grip, they both collapsed into the muddy ground breathing heavily as the rain continued to lighten. Vernon wiped some dirt from Charlene's face. She stared confused into his eyes, as if paralyzed by his affectionate touch.

Only inches away from her face, Vernon slowly moved in closer, expecting her to stop him at any moment. Gently he kissed her on the cheek. Yielding to his touch, she allowed him to kiss her other cheek, her forehead, her bottom lip.

Pulling back, she ran her fingers through his muddy hair to study him.

"Is this nice enough for you?"

"Absolutely."

Wrapping her legs around his waist, Charlene pulled Vernon in close to wrestle around in the mud again - this time acknowledging they would both be the victors as they slowly began exploring each other's bodies.

PULLING ON A full-length silky white dressing gown, Paula stumbled to her front door.

"What now?" she grumbled to herself as the doorbell persistently chimed.

Unbolting the latch, she saw Philippe standing there, bursting with excitement.

"You weren't still in bed?"

"Yes, and unless you have some good news for a change, I'm going straight back."

"Well my Sleeping Beauty, it looks like your Prince Charming has arrived just in time," he beamed, holding up a DVD disk.

"What's that?"

"Don't I get a cup of coffee first?"

"Yeah, sure, whatever. Come in."

"Well, aren't we the grumble-bum this morning?"

"Don't start, Philippe. I'm not in the mood."

She went to the kitchen and cursed herself for not having put on the percolator an hour earlier. Then she remembered why. She was out of fresh coffee. Urgh! That meant they'd have to drink instant. She hated instant coffee. Oh well.

The designer kettle whistled its readiness a moment later and Paula joined her friend in the living room with two steaming hot mugs. She sat on the couch and started absentmindedly playing with her DVD remote.

"You know how the police said all our security cameras were switched off on the night of the robbery?" Philippe began.

"Don't remind me."

"Well, I've just discovered that wasn't exactly true."

"What?"

"While I was at the gallery this morning, I thought I'd reset the combination on our wall safe's memory chip. You know, considering the last one is no good to us anymore. Anyway all of a sudden I remembered that this particular model of safe has its own hidden camera that operates whenever its door is open."

"So?"

"So I downloaded all the footage it had recorded since we installed it last year, onto a laser disk."

"And?"

"Let's just say, it's very interesting viewing."

He put the DVD into Paula's machine, took the remote from her and set it playing. Filling the screen of Paula's huge television, Philippe's face appeared over and over as he daily put the safety deposit box in the safe.

"Oh my God! Bad hair day or what?" he covered his eyes in mock horror.

"Come on, Philippe!"

"Alright, alright, don't get your knickers in a knot! I do do a lot of banking you know."

Again and again a similar picture repeated itself in fast motion.

"Me, me, me, me, me, ah here we go!"

Looking quite drunk, in his zebra suit, Philippe sloppily stacked piles of money into the safe, covering up the camera.

"Oh, great," Paula complained.

"Have patience, my pet."

After the safe door was closed, it reopened and the contents were dragged out and put into a sack by someone in a ski mask.

"This is no good. We still don't know who it is."

"Shhhh! Keep watching!"

Fast-forwarding again, the DVD showed the whole gallery clearly through the safe's security camera lens. Someone else in a ski mask appeared. The two robbers gradually emptied the whole gallery's contents into a black van parked out the front. After all the paintings were removed, one of them lifted the office filing cabinet with a trolley and it too was taken out to the van.

"Unbelievable," Paula said, horrified.

"But wait, there's more!"

Having totally cleaned out the gallery, the two thieves closed the van's doors and re-entered. After a quick look around to make sure they hadn't left any clues, the smaller robber grabbed the larger one and kissed him passionately through his mask.

"You've got to be joking," Paula gasped.

Kissing her back, the two robbers speedily undressed each other on Philippe's desk.

"Oh my God!"

"I know. Remind me to have my desk fumigated, will you?"

Totally intertwined in each other's bodies, wearing nothing but their ski masks, the couple started to make love on the desk. In the heat of the moment their masks came off, revealing Lisa Mendoza and Harbens Punjarb!

"No way!" Paula yelled.

"Yes way! See, she is human. Look at that cellulite."

"They're in it together!"

"That's certainly one way of putting it! Now, let me just fast forward this a bit, because frankly their stamina makes me feel a little inadequate."

Speeding through the tape's sexy material, Philippe stopped after the pair's obviously exhilarating climax. Lisa and Harbens climbed off the desk, redressed in their black overalls and ski masks, and exited the gallery before Lisa added her *piece de resistance*. Pulling out a brick from the front seat of the van, she hurled it though the front glass doors, shattering them instantly.

"Well, what do you think?" Philippe cheered.

"I'm speechless!"

"A shoe-in to win "America's Funniest Home Videos", or what?"

"We've got to get this over to the police a.s.a.p.!"

"One step ahead of you, babe. All they have to do now is find them."

BURSTING THROUGH the door of a cheap motel, Harbens, clad in a garishly shiny blue suit, carried Lisa, who wore a very revealing white wedding dress, across the threshold, laughing ecstatically.

"I love you, Mr. Punjarb!"

"I love you too, Mrs. Punjarb!"

"Lisa Punjarb? Oh, no, no, no! That will never do, I'm keeping Mendoza!"

Kissing her neck passionately, Harbens lay her on the bed.

"Whatever you say, my Puerto Rican princess!"

"Take me now, my pappadum prince!"

"Just let me take off this monkey suit and I'll be right back."

"Come here, let me!"

Grabbing him by the belt, Lisa hungrily pulled him to her body and started madly tearing off his clothes. Surrounding them were all of Harbens' paintings, carefully wrapped up in bubble paper and cardboard.

"Stop, stop, stop!"

"Why?" she pouted.

"Wait, my sexy little Spanish fly. I have to shower first."

"I don't care! I love your stink, your sweat, your ooouuhhh!"

Again she ravaged him.

"No, baby-cakes, listen! I gotta take a dump!"

Instantly losing her passion, Lisa pushed him away.

"Eww! Do you have to be so graphic?"

"I tried not to be, but you're so damn persistent!"

"Okay, go! But hurry, I'm burning up!"

Giving her one last fiery kiss, he pulled himself away and shut the bathroom door behind him.

Frustrated that she didn't get what she wanted, Lisa flopped back on the bed, picked up the phone and dialed the airport.

"Hello? I'd just like to confirm my flight to Puerto Rico. Yes, two tickets one way."

Sitting on the toilet, brushing his teeth, Harbens hummed to himself happily.

"Yes, Mumma," Lisa shrieked into the phone. "The big house on the corner that that drug dealer used to own - before he was shot. Of course, there'll be enough room for the whole family! Harbens? Don't worry about him, he does what I say."

Singing in the shower, Harbens worked himself up into quite a lather. He rinsed off, towel dried, put on some cheap aftershave and donned a leopard print g-string. After admiring himself in the mirror, he threw open the door and attempted to look seductive. The sight that met his eyes made him quiver. Lisa was lying on the bed covered in a blanket of dollar bills.

Diving on her hungrily, the pair rolled around in the money, kissing and laughing. Wearing very skimpy lingerie, Lisa straddled him and proceeded to throw handfuls of money into the air.

"Is this enough to get your film career going?"

"What career? Who cares about a career? We can live in luxury without needing to lift a finger now!"

She lowered herself down his body, trying not to cough on the overpowering smell of the aftershave, and was about to take him to heaven when the motel door was kicked open and an FBI SWAT team stormed in.

"Get down on the ground! Now!"

"Move!"

Dragging them off the bed, Lisa and Harbens were pushed to the floor and handcuffed.

"What the hell are you doing?" she yelled.

"Lisa Mendoza, Harbens Punjarb, you are both under arrest for grand theft and conspiracy to pervert the course of justice."

Lifting them up, the FBI agents escorted the conspirators out into the open.

"What are you talking about?" Lisa protested, as motel guests emerged to see what all the commotion was about.

Some turned away in embarrassment, while others giggled at the sight of the sexy Spanish senorita and the scrawny artist handcuffed and being led away in their underwear. One quick-thinking tourist reached for his camera, snapping the picture knowing some network would pay for the shot.

"You have the right to remain silent," the FBI told them. "If you give up this right, anything you say can and will be used against you in a court of law."

"This is a mistake! We've been framed," Harbens told them.

"You have a right to an attorney. If you cannot afford an attorney, one will be appointed for you."

Harbens was taken in one direction while Lisa was taken in the other.

"No! He's my husband! He's my husband! I wanna be with my husband!"

The remaining agents swooped on Harbens' paintings and carried them out of the motel to be returned to their rightful owners, as Lisa bit her handler and tried to break free.

"It wasn't me!" she yelled. "I didn't do anything. You're making a terrible mistake. Why won't anyone listen to me?"

Chapter 7

The afternoon sun had pushed away all signs of rain. Vernon stirred, stretched and yawned before realizing he was in bed alone. He walked out of Charlene's container home, shielding his eyes against the sun, to discover all his clothes had been hung up to dry. There was a note pegged to his shirt:

Thanks for everything - sorry I couldn't be there to say goodbye - had to go into town for supplies, and didn't want to wake you – Charlene & Shaka.

"Sure you didn't," he smiled.

He got dressed, determined this would not be the last time he saw this modest home, and returned to Matapula to say his farewells.

He was loading his luggage into his jeep when Sully approached him.

"Leaving so soon?"

"I'm afraid so."

"I thought you were here for at least another week yet."

"Yeah, me too. Unfortunately, I came up with my elephant solution way too quick, so now the company wants to send me to India."

"That's too bad. You didn't manage to bag any game either, did you?"

"Oh well, maybe I'll have better luck in India."

"Oh, Laurie asked me to get you to drop by his office before you leave."

"I'd like to but…"

"It'll only take a minute."

Realizing he would look suspicious if he didn't comply, Vernon agreed.

The office door was open, but he thought it appropriate to knock anyway as Laurie seemed deep in thought.

"Come in. Oh, Vincent. Take a seat."

Dressed in an old-fashioned hunting safari suit, Laurie was sitting behind a huge mahogany desk, drinking whisky. His office was unsurprisingly filled with hunting trophies.

"Sully said you wanted to see me?"

"Yes, yes. Didn't want you running off before I had a chance to share a final drink with you."

"It'll have to be a quick one."

"That's right, you're flying out tonight, aren't you? On the rocks, or straight?"

Having dropped ice in his own glass, Laurie held some over Vernon's in a pair of monkey paw tongs.

"No ice, thanks."

"Cool enough, eh? Anyway, I was a bit concerned you weren't getting your money's worth here, considering you've been away from us on business nearly every second day. So, I gave that hotel of yours a call to see if we could sort something out. When they informed me they hadn't seen much of you either, I called your bosses at Bell South."

"Really?"

"Yes - and they were most helpful."

Vernon remained impassive, but ready to strike.

"It seems you're quite an invaluable asset to them. Anyway, I asked them to cut you a bit of slack, you know, so you could at least take home a portrait of yourself in front of a trophy kill, but alas no, they were quite adamant that your services are needed elsewhere. Pity, 'coz there's a hunt I know you'd be interested in."

"Is that so?"

"Yes. Oh, and before I forget, I want you to take a look at these…"

Laurie pulled out a huge photo album, and passed it to Vernon.

"What's this?"

"I call it my "file of fame". It's my private collection of Polaroids - some of the wealthiest and most influential men in the world, who just happen to have stayed here. I got presidents, media giants, politicians, movie stars, members of royal families, billionaires - you name it, they're in there!"

"Impressive," Vernon conceded, thumbing through the album, and wondering how he could take it with him.

"Obviously I can never display any of them publicly, but I do enjoy showing them off to fellow hunters, like yourself."

"Thanks for the privilege."

"I bet that Charlene Tynsworth would love to get her hands on these beauties, eh?"

"Who?"

"I'm surprised you haven't run into her. She's our local animal activist and major pain in the ass. I swear that bitch won't rest until she runs me, and every one of my colleagues, out of business."

"That's too bad. There must be some way to shut her up?"

"Oh, there is. I'll set Arnie onto her! When I can find her," he said sarcastically, refilling his glass. "Another one?"

"No thanks."

"Oh, and here's some new snaps. You're gonna love these."

Sliding a manila folder across the desk to Vernon, Laurie observed his every movement closely, waiting in lurid anticipation.

Opening the folder, Vernon saw photographs of Tex and his fellow hunters standing proudly in front of their kills. It all seemed pretty run of the mill stuff, until he came to the end of the pile. Suddenly the blood drained from his face. The next photos were of him and Charlene making love in the mud.

"So, I see you finally sorted out your love life."

Realizing the game was up, Vernon sprang to his feet, only to be stopped by Lertz who, quick as lightning, leapt out of the shadows and wrapped a wire choker around Vernon's throat.

"Did you really think I'd just let anyone come in here to expose my life and destroy my career?"

As Vernon struggled against Lertz's incredible power, Laurie punched him square in his face.

"You're good, I'll give you that. My boys did a major search on you and came up with nothing. So, although we still don't know which organization you're with, we know who you're working for now, don't we?"

Picking up the photograph of Charlene, Laurie waved it in front of Vernon's bright-red choking face.

"We've been looking for her new campsite for some time now. Thanks for leading us right to her!"

Picking up a gun, Laurie slung an ammunition belt over his shoulder and prepared to leave.

"I'd love to stay and watch you die, Mr. Nash, or whatever your name is. But Arnie and I have a date with a certain little lady."

No matter how desperately Vernon struggled to get at Laurie, he found himself frustratingly totally powerless.

"But don't worry," Laurie taunted him. "I'll be leaving you in Lertz's capable hands. Cheerio."

"Nooooo," Vernon managed to scream, as Laurie left the office.

Blissfully unaware of what was happening at Matupula, and still feeling warm and fuzzy from her morning's lovemaking, Charlene made herself a cup of tea and dropped a bowl of milk on the floor for Shaka.

As dusk descended on Zimbabwe, she decided there really wasn't much else to do; she'd have an early night.

Dropping down forward, Vernon managed to flip Lertz over the desk, winding him. After only a second to catch his breath, the robot-like killing machine was ready to attack again.

Meeting in hand-to-hand combat, a violent battle exploded between two equally-matched, highly-trained killers, each especially motivated and extremely focused on destroying the other.

Whipping out his metal wire again, Lertz managed to double loop it around Vernon's neck. Desperately gasping for air and grappling around on Laurie's desk, Vernon found a warthog tusk next to an open steel strong box. He propelled the eight-inch curved natural dagger backwards into Lertz's eye socket.

The thrust was too sudden to cause pain, but the force of the blow, and the shock of the loss of sight in one eye, sent Lertz reeling back, loosening his grip.

Pushing off the desk, Vernon drove his opponent backwards, impaling him on a pair of kudu horns that hung on the wall. His remaining eye opened wide in terror before, gurgling blood, Lertz's gauged body fell limp.

Sitting up in bed, Charlene found she couldn't sleep. She kept reliving what had happened that morning over and over in her head, wondering if she would ever see Vernon again. It was ridiculous, of course. She knew that. He'd completed his mission, had his fun, and was probably thirty thousand feet in the air on his way back to the States by now, already planning who would next be in need of "Pest Control".

Trying to shake the images from her mind, she picked up a book to read by oil lantern light.

Vernon bent double, trying to catch his breath. He was covered in blood, but didn't realize until he tried to stand up that some of it was his own. He winced, grabbing his side, knowing he had to pack that wound if he was going to effective in the fight he knew was yet to come.

A native worker ambled into the office, took one look at Lertz, and instantly retreated to alert the whole lodge.

"Shit," Vernon muttered to himself.

He grabbed a pump action shotgun from Laurie's display cabinet and loaded it, shoving spare ammo into his pockets. He used Laurie's whisky to quickly sterilize his wound – it stung like hell. He then packed it with the remaining ice and shreds he tore from his shirt, put the photo album in Laurie's strong box, and prepared for battle.

Running out into the compound, the native worker's panicked cries caused pandemonium among his fellow employees. Stumbling forward, Daniels left the outdoor bar to see what all the racket was about.

"What the fuck's going on?"

A flurry of native dialect was jabbered in high-pitched, excited tones.

Even though he only understood every second word, Daniels soon got the gist of the situation. He handed out weapons to the remaining native workers, as well as the drunken hunters, and gave one simple order.

"Shoot to kill, men!"

Vernon ran for his jeep only to find the hood open, the distributor cap missing and all the tyres deflated. He tossed the metal box in with his luggage, as a shotgun blast ripped through the jeep's roof, narrowly missing his head.

Instinctively swinging around, Vernon returned fire, blowing away two native workers.

He ran around to the back of the lodge, where he was met with another barrage of bullets forcing him to hit the dirt behind a tour bus, from where he could shoot back under cover.

Seeming to react to Daniels' shouting, native workers surrounded the tour bus.

Vernon removed what was left of his shirt and shoved it into the open petrol tank, grabbing hold of a nearby fire torch to set it alight.

Jumping around the corner brandishing a crossbow, a native worker was shot dead before he could take aim.

In the time it took for the tour bus to detonate, Vernon blasted away the remainder of the native workers and double-timed it to the shooting range.

Cowering behind the storeroom counter, the drunken hunters loaded their high-powered weapons.

Vernon grabbed another fire torch and hurled it into the storeroom, instantly causing an inferno. Leaping out of the side door just in time, Daniels only narrowly avoided being perforated like a rifle-range target by all the live ammunition that subsequently ignited. The hunters were not so fortunate. As the storeroom erupted in a fireworks display worthy of the 4th of July, the hunters took flight before thudding lifelessly on the dirt.

Heading for the only functional jeep left, Daniels fumbled for his keys while shrapnel flew all around him. It was a mistake.

Appearing as if by magic, Vernon caught Daniels in the throat, snapping his head back. Ignoring the fire that was raging out of control behind him, he reached down to pry the jeep's keys out of Daniels' dead hand. He was about to jump in when a huge explosion knocked him unconscious. Vernon hit the ground hard.

LIGHT FROM Charlene's campfire lazily illuminated her jeep, creating an elongated shadow over the surrounding bush. Inside her container home, Charlene sat up in bed sweating profusely, still trying to convince herself she was concentrating on the book she wasn't reading. Suddenly Shaka woke from a deep sleep and growled. It was a deep, throaty rumble, followed by a series of short high-pitched barks.

"Don't worry, boy. It's probably just a passing kudu."

Not so easily convinced, Shaka stood at attention.

Outside a pair of black boots stepped out of a truck and walked around the back to unhinge a latch.

Charlene placed a bookmark in her book, put it down, and grabbed her pillow and blanket to head outside.

"Another night in nature's cooking pot, eh Shaka? Come on, if we stay in here any longer we'll melt."

Safely on top of the truck's roof, with rifles in hand, Laurie, Tex, Sully, and two other hunters sat ready to watch the show. Climbing up next to them, two native workers joined the party in time to witness Charlene step out of her container with Shaka at her side.

"This is gonna be good," Laurie leered.

Responding to Laurie's signal, the native workers quietly slid up a cage door and Arnie jumped out.

"Dinner is served," Lawrence Watson announced.

Shaka started to growl again.

"What is it, Shaka? What's got you so spooked?"

Stalking closer and closer to Charlene, Arnie stopped and crouched down to pounce.

Convinced Shaka was trying to tell her something, Charlene surveyed her surroundings eventually noticing two huge eyes glowing in the bushes.

"Oh no."

Spotting what Charlene had seen, Shaka charged straight for Arnie.

"Shaka! No!"

Pouncing out from the darkness, Arnie swatted the brave little dog like a fly. Shaka hit the ground yelping, and fell silent.

"Shaka!"

Cheering in the distance, Charlene's evil audience couldn't have been having more fun.

"Go Arnie!"

"Back home we'd pay premium dollars for a show like this!"

The big lion charged at Charlene. She grabbed a shovel to defend herself, striking her attacker with a force that stunned even her. For a moment Arnie was dazed. But only a moment. The heavy cat soon clambered to his feet and saw his prey scrambling to the safety of her jeep.

Struggling with the latch, to her horror Charlene discovered the door was jammed. She ran to the container instead.

Slamming its door shut behind her, Charlene thought she was safe until Arnie's paw slashed in before she could latch the door down. She forced all her weight against the door, but with a hundred and eighty kilos of angry lion on the other side she was fighting a losing battle.

Laurie and his cronies rocked with laughter, as Charlene was knocked off her feet and Arnie charged in with claws thrusting.

She blocked his attacks with whatever she could find, tossing chairs, books, whatever came to hand.

"Quick! Get down there and lock the door," Laurie ordered his native staff.

Looking at each other in fear, the two native workers seemed none too keen to obey their master.

Inside the container, Charlene lifted her bed and hid behind it. Furiously, Arnie ripped into the mattress, which came apart effortlessly in a shower of feathers under his claws.

Outside, the native workers had apparently decided that Laurie was far more terrifying than Arnie, and crept up to the container to lock it shut from the outside. However, the commotion inside was sufficient to change their minds. In the bat of an eyelid they turned tail, running into the night.

"What the fuck are they doing?"

"Get back here, you cowards!"

"Sully! Get down there and finish the job!"

"Me?"

"Well, shit!" yelled Tex. "We ain't going down there son, we're paying customers!"

The other hunters nodded in agreement with Tex.

"I thought you said it was supposed to look like an accident," Sully reasoned.

"It will," Laurie assured him.

"Not if the door's shut from the outside."

"So, we open the door, shoot the fucker, and say we got here too late to save her. Simple."

"I dunno."

"Get down there and shut that fuckin' door, or you can find yourself a new employer!"

Given no choice, Sully reluctantly complied.

Fighting against Arnie as best she could, Charlene pushed the mattress forward on top of the lion and headed for the open door. WHAM! It slammed closed.

"No!"

Sully held the container door latch firmly down, trapping Charlene inside. Sighing with relief that he'd accomplished his task safely, he nervously began to chuckle to himself.

"Let me out! Please! Let me out!"

Temporarily held underneath the mattress, Arnie furiously slashed around to escape, knocking over the oil lantern in the process. Instantly the container's contents erupted in flames.

Acting on instinct and adrenalin, Charlene grabbed her keys, flipped her bed base over to protect herself, and escaped through a hatch in the rear. Tearing at the bed base, Arnie quickly pulled it aside and scrambled after her.

Unable to believe his eyes, Sully watched as Charlene sprinted past him, while he was still holding the door latch shut.

"What?" he mumbled.

Turning to see where Charlene had come out from, Sully eyes opened in terror as Arnie pounced on him, savagely attacking his tormentor. He remembered only too well all those beatings he'd received at this man's hand, and while Arnie had learned to hate all men, this was one he hated with a particular vengeance.

"Shit," one of the hunters cried, just before he threw up.

Arnie ripped the top of Sully's skull open with one swipe of his paw. He was still alive and aware of the hot saliva mingling with his own blood as Arnie got a taste of his sadistic jailer's brain.

"She's getting away," Tex yelled, apparently unconcerned at the terrible fate that had just befallen Sully.

"Not if I can help it," Laurie said firmly, aiming his gun to shoot at Charlene as she ran to her jeep.

Ducking down to avoid the bullet, Charlene dropped her keys in the dirt.

"There she is," Tex yelled. "No damn fool bitch is gonna expose my private activities on national television. Get back here you scheming piece of crap."

"I got her," Laurie growled.

Having made a meal of Sully, Arnie turned to finish off whomever else he could lay his paws on.

"Wait. Here he comes," Tex whispered loudly.

Taking her only chance, Charlene picked up her keys, opened her passenger side door and slid in. Reaching for the ignition, she suddenly felt a vice-like grip on her leg as Arnie hooked a swiping claw into her ankle and dragged her back out.

Watching Charlene screaming in agony and terror, the hunters began laughing again in blood-lusting euphoria. They were far too pleased with themselves to notice another jeep approaching at breakneck speed. Tex was rolling so hard he nearly fell off the roof. It was only in steadying himself that he looked around.

"What the hell?"

He soon realized the other jeep's driver had jumped from the moving vehicle, leaving it on a collision course with the hunter's truck. It hit hard, exploding into a ball of searing flames and throwing all the occupants down to the ground.

The big lion loosened his grip on Charlene, in turning to see what the noise was. Having landed only feet from him, Arnie pounced on one of the hunters, tearing at his throat. Muted by the attack and already mortally wounded, the hunter fumbled in a tangle of arms and legs, trying to hit the angry lion with his bare fists. It was barely more annoying than the buzzing of flies to Arnie, who quickly finished off his prey with a bone-snapping crunch of his jaws.

Instinctively knowing his time had come, and an opportunity like this would likely never present itself again, Arnie turned his attention to Tex, catching him on the arm and knocking his rifle out of reach. Tex fell backwards in shock. The remaining hunter screamed in terror which, luckily for the Senator, attracted Arnie's attention.

The big lion left Tex and jumped on the cowardly hunter instead, digging his claws into the two-legs' chubby back and biting down.

"Help me! Somebody help me," he squealed.

Horrified at how the sequence of events had turned against him, and worried about losing another paying customer, Laurie rushed to the hunter's aid, planting a bullet into Arnie's hindquarter. The force knocked the big lion sideways but did little to slow him down. Confused, Arnie scrambled back to his feet, noticing Charlene had managed to pull herself back into the jeep, this time closing the door behind her.

Laurie took aim again, shooting out Charlene's passenger side window. That was all the opening Arnie needed. He reached in swiping at Charlene, slashing painfully into her flesh.

The situation was too serious to be amusing any longer. Although Laurie was half tempted to gloat he could see Arnie was not in a position to inflict a fatal blow. He fired again, striking at the jeep's windscreen and blasting it open.

Undeterred by explosions or bullets, in a frenzy of pain and revenge, functioning with a mind that was demented and twisted from his years of torture, Arnie had only one objective – kill all the two-legs. Being given an opening by Laurie, he pounced onto the jeep's hood feverishly swiping at Charlene who could do nothing but look on in horror.

Laurie cautiously allowed himself to relax a little, reveling in the show, when he was king hit from behind, slamming him into the ground. Cracking him in the face with the butt of his own rifle, Vernon wasted no time in disabling Charlene's would-be assassin. Without pausing for breath, he lifted the rifle and blasted at Arnie, knocking him off the jeep.

"No! Don't kill him! Don't kill him!"

Ignoring Charlene's pleas, Vernon continued to pump the remains of the ammunition into the tortured and brutalized lion. But living up to his namesake, the Terminator of a creature still managed to struggle to his feet with his dying breaths to attack again.

Having run out of ammo, Vernon was forced to use the empty rifle as a weapon. If he could have laughed, and had he been in the mood, Arnie might have found this quite amusing, as he effortlessly swiped it away. He was battle-torn and weak, but the king of the jungle was still a formidable opponent and not prepared to quit before he'd taken one more two-leg with him.

Wrestling the lion as though he was Tarzan, Vernon held back Arnie's snapping jaws with one hand while sliding out his hunting knife with the other, quickly burying it in Arnie's ribs.

Crawling painfully out of the jeep, Charlene took a deep intake of air and steadied herself against her vehicle.

"Stop! Stop, Vernon! Please stop," she cried as loud as she could.

But her appeal fell on deaf ears. Vernon was doing what he did best, and he was on automatic pilot. Repeatedly he stabbed into Arnie's flesh until all the torture and pain in this poor demented creature's life came to a bloody end.

"No! No! No," Charlene sobbed.

Pushing Arnie's dead carcass aside, Vernon staggered to his feet, covered from head to toe in blood. His eyes were wild. He surveyed the perimeter for further threats.

Dizzy from her own injuries, her eyes stinging with tears, Charlene was barely able to focus.

"Shit! Help! Help," Tex suddenly called.

The second hunter Arnie had taken a chunk out of started crawling towards a rifle. Straddling him from above, Vernon leant over, sleeper held his neck, and snapped it like a dry twig.

"Oh my God," Tex cried. "Shit! Somebody help me!"

Vernon turned on him with the burning fiery rage of the depths of Hell itself.

"No. No! Get away from me, you fuckin' maniac!" Quaking like the rattle at the tail end of a venomous snake, Tex crawled under the remains of the truck for protection.

"How do *you* like it, Senator? How does it feel to be the hunted one?" Vernon called threateningly.

Tex bowed his head under the truck and started to cry like a baby. "Have mercy! Please! I'm begging you!"

Dropping down, Vernon grabbed Tex's heel with cobra striking speed and dragged him out from under the truck.

"No! No! Please! No!"

Holding Tex by the throat, Vernon was about to bury his knife in when sensed someone behind him. Spinning around in time to register Laurie's face, Vernon received a blow from his nemesis's Bowie hunting knife.

"You should have killed me when you had the chance!"

Vernon was down, but not out. In a heartbeat he was on his feet again, stalking Laurie in a circle.

"I never told you why the SAS kicked me out, did I?"

Vernon remained silent and focused, yet Laurie still managed to catch him with a sneaky jab.

"I stabbed my drill sergeant to death in a knife fight." Laurie leered, like a wolf baring teeth.

"That's it," Tex bellowed. "Kill him! Kill that son-of-a-bitch!"

Slashing and dodging each other, both men knew this was a fight to the death.

"Kill him Laurie, and a million bucks is all yours," Tex urged desperately.

"Oh no," Laurie called back. "This one's for me."

Occasionally getting tagged by Laurie's blade, Vernon dived forward in an attempt to gain control, catching Laurie's knife arm at the wrist. But Laurie was equally as well-trained as Vernon and simultaneously caught Vernon by his wrist with his other hand.

"Not too bad for an old guy, eh?"

"Not good enough," Vernon rumbled, although he was silently admitting he had apparently underestimated his deadly opponent's strength.

"I'm gonna hang your fucking head on my wall!"

Dropping his own blade to the ground, Vernon used his free hand to twist back Laurie's wrist, snapping it at the bone. Speedily ripping the Bowie knife from his enemy's limp hand, Vernon spun around slicing Laurie across the throat. As he reached his unbroken hand to his bloodied throat, Vernon thrust the blade up into Laurie's chest.

"Not today," he told the Lodge owner, hugging his body as it became as floppy as a rag doll.

Laurie stared back into Vernon's face in shock, before his eyes rolled hideously into the back of his head.

Dumping his latest victim to the ground, Vernon turned back to Tex with the look of a maniacal murderer.

"No! No! I didn't mean it! I'll give you the million! Ten million! A billion! Whatever you want! No! No…"

"No!" Charlene shouted.

Charlene! He'd momentarily forgotten all about her. God, what had he turned into? He turned his back on Tex and flew to her side.

Taking his chance, the cowardly senator fell over himself bolting off into the bushes in a frantic panicked escape.

"Get away from me – you – murderer!" she sobbed, pushing Vernon away with what little strength she had. "Shaka? Where's Shaka?"

Before he could attempt an answer, she passed out. He scooped her up tenderly and placed her in her jeep, only then looking around to see Shaka flat on the dirt.

With blood in his own eyes, it was all Vernon could do to see the road as the jeep careered through the night.

"Stay with me, Charlene! Stay with me!"

It seemed an eternity before he burst through the double doors of Bulawayo's medical center, where Charlene was instantly rushed into emergency surgery.

Prevented from following any further, Vernon was led away by a nurse who tended to his own wounds. Knowing he could do no more for Charlene at this point, he submitted to the nurse's ministrations, looking up at the hospital wall clock. It read: 7.38pm.

When the surgeon next looked up at the emergency room clock it read: 11.17pm. He sadly covered over a dead body with a white sheet. After giving a nod to two orderlies, they took the corpse to the morgue.

Walking with heavy disappointment, the doctor left a nurse to clean up. Metal instruments clanged noisily in the deathly silence. With numb automatic efficiency the nurse continued with her duties, before opening a curtain around another bed.

Behind the curtain, Charlene was sleeping peacefully, bandaged on almost every part of her body. Vernon patted her forehead gently with a damp cloth.

"You're safe now. I've just got one last thing to do, and I'll be right back."

He swept a stray piece of hair off her face, kissed her on the forehead and walked out.

STILL RUNNING into the night, Tex was desperately trying to get a signal on cell phone.

"Hello? Hello! Can anybody hear me? SOS! S.O.S!"

Injured, out of condition and blind with fear, Tex stopped for a breath. When he looked up again he was certain he must have slipped into some B-grade nightmare flick. Prowling around him in a quickening pace was a hungry pride of lions.

"No. No! No…"

His last cry was drowned out by the roar of a family of big cats devouring their evening meal.

"OH MY GOD!" Paula shouted into her portable phone, pacing the gallery floor.

"It can't be that bad," Philippe assured her. "You'll get your credit rating back."

"No, that was Vernon. Charlene was nearly mauled to death by a lion last night."

"Oh my God. Is she alright?"

"She's lost a lot of blood, but he said she should pull through."

"And how is he?"

"He could have his head cut off and he'd brush it off as a minor scratch," she scoffed.

"Still in awe of the hero, eh?"

She ignored the question.

"Kinda makes you wonder if we're doing the right thing, doesn't it? I mean after all the trouble we've gone through, Charlene goes and gets herself attacked by a lion!"

Philippe placed his hands on her shoulders. "You know what they say – no good deed ever goes unpunished."

"Oh Philippe. I don't know what I … "

"… would do with out me? Yes, I know, I know."

She hugged him tightly, trying to hold back tears that wanted to flow for a thousand different reasons.

CHARLENE WAS STILL sleeping when Vernon returned. He didn't remember how long it had been since he'd slept himself; too long. He tried to force his eyes open by getting up and pacing, but his entire body felt like a dead weight. He had to sit down. He squelched into a chair and immediately his head fell forward and quickly snapped back again. His vision was a bit blurry. He strained his back muscles straight and rubbed his eyes. Suddenly Charlene stirred.

"Hey. We thought we'd lost you there for a while."

Charlene looked around and reached for a glass of water. He was instantly on his feet to assist.

"I'm fine. I can manage."

"You gave us all quite a scare. I bet there aren't many people who can claim they survived a lion attack."

At the mention of the lion, Charlene sank into despair.

"If you're worried about the lion, don't be. After all it had been through, I think it's better off dead."

"What would you know?"

Well that got him a long way – not. Change the subject, yes, that was a good ploy.

"I got Bricks to check out what the local police think happened last night. At this stage it appears they're blaming a rebel militant group who've been carrying out anti-white protest killings in the area. Because I've been working under an alias it should be virtually impossible for them to connect us with it, but I've still organized a charter plane to get us out of here, as soon as you're well enough to travel."

"Forget it. I'm not going anywhere with you."

"Listen, I understand you may or may not like my company at the moment, but I do think you should at least come back to the States with me until all this blows over and it's safe again."

Sitting up in bed with a new-found strength, Charlene locked her eyes on Vernon.

"Safe? Safe for who? When has a lawless country like Zimbabwe ever been safe for anyone? And what about the wildlife? Who's gonna keep them safe? You? It's men like you that they should be afraid of!"

"Hey, I saved your life last night, Charlene."

"I would rather have died, than be responsible for yet another dead animal! Who says my life is any more important than that lion's?"

"I do! I love you!" Even as the words left his lips, he couldn't believe he'd just said that. He thought about it a moment longer. Was it true? Did he? "I've loved you since the first moment I met you."

"You love me?" she spat. "After seeing what you did last night, I doubt you even have a heart!"

"You know I do, Charlene. And somewhere inside of you, you have feelings for me too; otherwise you'd never have let me in."

"You're a soulless killing machine! If you think I could ever love a man like you, you're deluded!"

Her words cut him deeper than any wound. “You really mean that, don’t you?”

She rolled over, turning way from him. “You just make sure you finish your job and get that footage out to the world, or all of this has been for nothing.”

“I guess this is good-bye then?”

He received no answer. Convinced that silence was her way of telling him to leave her life forever, he heavily got up and walked out.

As his footsteps faded into the distance she tossed and turned in bed, hugging her pillow.

Chapter 8

Boeing 747 flight number 863 rose into the African sky, framed by a fiery red-orange sunset. Battle scarred, bruised, and yes, even heartbroken, Vernon stared out of his window at the immense, ancient, mystical, magical, brutal, magnificent land that Charlene called Mother Africa.

Sitting in her wheelchair looking out of the hospital window, Charlene turned to a noise behind her. Standing there smiling with a row of dazzlingly white teeth, was the native farmer who owned the donkey she'd helped. He was carrying a huge picnic basket, which he placed on her lap. Slowly, hardly containing his excitement, the farmer pulled back the cloth covering to reveal an almost mummified yet quite alive -

"Shaka!"

Tears of joy streamed down her face. Gently she stroked the little dog's ears as he licked her nose. On closer inspection, she noticed dog tags hanging around his neck – Vernon's.

"Mister Vernon took Shaka to the vet after he was sure you were going to be alright," the farmer explained. "Apparently he threatened the vet's life if he didn't save the little fella. The vet brought him to me."

Charlene pressed her lips together in a half smile, half sob.

PUSHING A LUGGAGE trolley through the LAX arrivals lounge, Vernon spotted Paula racing towards him. She flew into his arms, holding him as though she never intended to let him out of her sight again. "Oh boy," he thought. "Why can't life be as straight forward as combat?"

After making some appropriate comments, and even more appropriate excuses, he hurried back to his office and the sanctuary of male companionship that was generally very uncomplicated. Unpacking his bags, he showed Bricks and Jackson the video footage, top-secret files, and Laurie's photo album. Bricks raised his eyebrows in amazement, totally speechless when he saw who the photos were of.

AS THE JUDGE brought his gavel down, Lisa and Harbens were taken away wearing handcuffs and orange correctional uniforms. She wriggled and screamed in fast-paced Spanish, while Harbens just followed his captors with a numb, shell-shocked expression on his face.

"You're the one who should be locked away," she screamed hysterically at the judge. "You crazy bastard! Can't you see what's happening here?"

"Bailiff," said the judge calmly. "Restrain that woman."

Equally calmly, the bailiff took a firm hold of Lisa who was lashing out at anyone she could, both verbally and physically.

"You can't do this!" she shouted.

"I assure you, I can," the judge told her sternly.

"Do something," Lisa pleaded, turning to her lawyer. She could see in his eyes he didn't even like her. She wasn't going to get any help there.

"My defense counsel is inept. I demand a retrial."

"You have the right to appeal."

"Appeal – yes!" she turned to her lawyer. "Appeal!"

"I don't think so," he answered simply. Packing away his papers, the lawyer's eyes fell on the far wall of the courtroom where a pile of Harbens' paintings were stacked with "Notice of Acquisition" stickers plastered prominently all over them.

NO MATTER what drama or triumph was playing out in the world, at Jerry's Deli the normal hum of the diners always buzzed in blissful oblivion of their fellow patrons. So it came as no surprise to Paula that she once again felt totally isolated, even in this throbbing crowd of people. She was experiencing a disquieting sense of *deja vu*. Sitting in the same booth she'd sat in when she first met Tom, she once again twiddled her straw in a glass of mineral water as she waited for him to arrive.

This time there were no embarrassing introductions at least. He simply slid into the seat opposite her, ordered a mineral water for himself, and sat stone-faced.

"What do you want - the good news, or the bad?" he asked.

"The good."

"All of my contacts in the media are going absolutely crazy over Vernon's material."

Paula clasped her hands to her face in delight. That was the main thing after all – the mission had been a success. The price had been high to be sure, and in every sense. But the objective had been achieved.

"And the bad?" she asked nervously, thinking he was going to say Vernon had left the country for six years.

"Not one of the networks is prepared to retract their defamatory reports about you."

Her hands fell limp to her sides. "Even though I've more than been proved innocent?"

"I'm afraid so. They're worried it could open a floodgate for all the others they've defamed for ratings over the years."

"Can't I sue?"

"Sure. But these corporations have enough resources to keep you in court until you're a little old lady."

"But they've destroyed my reputation! And after everything I've done."

"That's showbiz."

"That stinks! So what am I supposed to do now?"

"I'll tell you what, I'll make a couple more calls."

SIX WEEKS LATER, Paula had all but given up hope of ever getting back the social status she'd once enjoyed as one of Hollywood's most sought-after art suppliers. There wasn't even any point in putting the gallery up for sale as most of its value was in goodwill and there was precious little of that left. Instead, she decided to sign it over to Philippe, who fortunately hadn't been tarnished in the scandal, and let him build the business back up, paying her a percentage of what he made.

Vernon had offered to send clients of his who were interested in art to *Dante's Art Gallery*, but ever since, he'd been out of the country on some mission or another. Paula consoled herself in the fact that she still had her apartment in Beverly Hills, the mission had been an overwhelming success, and now she had time to work with Joan in her sanctuary. At least here she could contribute hands-on and make a difference, albeit a small one. Okay, so she'd sunk into social oblivion, and no one would ever know the part she played in the whole scheme of things, but so what? She was blessed with having at least two true friends in Joan and Philippe. And that, she reasoned, was two more than most people in Hollywood had.

Still, she did have one thing to look forward to. Joan had organized a get-together of everyone who had been involved with the mission, as a private celebration for those who really knew what went on behind the scenes. Charlene was coming from Zimbabwe to address a large audience, and Vernon had even said he'd join them at the dinner afterwards. Her heart skipped at the thought of seeing him again. She hadn't been to a beauty parlor in ages, but in honor of the special occasion she'd taken a day out and pampered herself from head to toe.

At 7pm the ballroom in the Los Angeles Hilton once again overflowed with delegates as Charlene took the podium.

"The graphic footage you've just witnessed is the same material we released to the worldwide media only a few short weeks ago. Since then, it has been broadcast in over fifty-eight countries around the globe. Public awareness of our cause is at an all-time high. Financial and moral support has flooded in like never before. And finally, the international hunting community has been forced to take notice of us."

The audience applauded.

"But we still have a long way to go," Joan added. "And the road will never be easy, but at least now the ball is rolling; and if we remain vigilant it has the potential to pick up momentum. It is up to us now to name and shame these hunters – boycott their businesses, don't vote for them when they run for office, and keep pressure on the US government to ban the import of ALL hunting trophies once and for all. Will you help us?"

The reaction from the crowd said it all. There was thunderous applause and a standing ovation for the two women who were now known the world over for risking everything to expose the truth.

Charlene smiled humbly as Joan gave her a huge hug for the world to see.

In the audience, sitting between Philippe and Vernon, Paula tried to hold back her tears. She was delighted with what had happened, pleased and proud for Joan and Charlene, but totally uncertain as to what the rest of her life held for her.

Both caring for her and sensing her anguish, Philippe and Vernon put their arms around her, touching each other as they did so. Philippe felt a quiver of desire rush through him, while Vernon pulled back his arm with the speed of a NASA space shuttle. Paula couldn't help but giggle.

After the formal presentation was over, the group of friends sat in a quiet cordoned off area of the a la carte restaurant. Philippe, Paula, Vernon, Tom and Charlene all respectfully listened to Joan praise them.

"You know, I look around this table tonight and see a group of people I am proud to call my friends."

Paula took Vernon's arm.

"All of you, in some way, have suffered and sacrificed for this cause and I thank you."

Charlene looked at Paula and Vernon, an unfamiliar pain striking sharply in her chest.

"But honestly, at the end of the day, you've got to ask yourself: what was it all for?"

Vernon glanced longingly towards Charlene, who turned away quickly.

"A tiny piece of information that is here today and gone tomorrow. But whatever you do, don't be discouraged by this. Because it was probably only a tiny piece of information that got deep inside all of your hearts in the first place, and look what you've been able to do."

Philippe tried to give his undivided attention to Joan, but couldn't help noticing the body language between Paula, Charlene and Vernon.

"They say it only takes one person to change the world. Well, imagine how many other hearts are out there right now, pumping with a new beat of compassion and inspiration, waiting to join us in changing that world!"

Raising their glasses, everyone at the table indicated their agreement with Joan.

"Hear, hear," Philippe cheered.

"It may not happen tomorrow, but I promise you, it *will* happen! What did one of those famous hunters say? Oh yes: "We will prevail!""

Everyone smirked, recognizing all too well at whom that reference was aimed.

"Bravo," Tom boomed.

"Oh, Joan, stop! You're going to make me cry," Paula stammered, burying her head into Vernon's shoulder.

That was about as much as Charlene could stand. She stood up and tried to leave.

"Are you alright, Charlene?" Joan asked.

"Yes, yes, I'm fine. But I have a plane to catch."

"Homesick already?"

"You could say that," Charlene flushed with embarrassment, thinking "sick" just about described it. In her hurry to escape she accidentally knocked over a chair at the end of the table. "Like Joan said," she fumbled. "Thank you everyone for all you've done. It's really made a difference." With that, she quickly left the room.

Not attempting to offer an explanation, Vernon hurriedly got up to follow her.

Paula looked towards Philippe, confused. He simply shrugged in reply.

"She'll be fine," Joan offered. "Charlene just finds it hard to display her emotions around humans, that's all."

She was already outside with her luggage when Vernon caught up with her.

"Charlene?"

She refused to look at him, not wanting him to see the redness in her eyes. "It didn't take you long," she said stingingly.

"What? Oh. It's not what you think."

"Tell that to Paula."

"Paula's a very special person, but…"

"Spare me the details. I really hope you'll be happy together. Truly."

"And what about you?"

"I stopped thinking about me a long time ago."

A taxi pulled up to the curb and Charlene swiftly climbed in. "LAX please."

"It doesn't have to be like this, Charlene."

"Yes it does," she snapped back, closing the door.

"Why?"

She took a deep breath and wound down her window. "What did you call it? That's right, "priorities". Drive on, please."

"Wait! What about the anti-poaching patrols? What about *those* priorities? You still need someone for that."

"I'll find someone."

"Charlene, don't leave like this. Please."

"Thank you for everything you've done – really – and thank you for Shaka. Goodbye Vernon. Drive on please."

At her command, the cab driver pulled his taxi away and she was finally able to let out the sobs she'd so valiantly been holding back.

"You alright, ma'am?"

"Just drive please," she whimpered.

"Okay, ma'am, but if you want to talk – "

"I don't."

Vernon could do little more than stare sadly after the disappearing cab.

"Hey," Paula said timidly from behind him.

"Hey," he replied despondently.

"You had quite an adventure together, didn't you?"

"You could say that."

"You can go after her - if you, you know, want to."

Vernon spun around to face her, clearly shocked. "You're amazing," he said tenderly.

"Thank you."

"Come on. Why don't we go back inside and join the others?"

"We?"

Still unwilling to say the words she desperately wanted to hear, Vernon turned to head inside, beckoning her to follow.

"Coming?" he called.

"Why not?" she muttered to herself.

Suddenly Philippe darted into the lobby. "Hey, has the party moved out here, or what? It's rude to leave a Hollywood legend on her own, you know!"

"I'm coming already," Paula shot back.

He could see she was hurting, and he could see Vernon was hurting - and dang it all, he missed Tom too! "Funny, isn't it?"

"What's that?" she asked.

"Here we are all congratulating ourselves on what a fantastic job we've done, and every one of us is suffering from a broken heart!"

"Irony," she readily agreed.

"Oh, I did forget to tell you something," he smiled cheekily.

"What's that?" she asked absentmindedly.

"Those calls Tom made – Oprah was looking for you today. She wants to devote a whole show to you!"

"What?"

"So who's the hero now?"

"Oprah? Really?"

"Yes, really!"

"Oh, Philippe!" she squealed, hurling herself into his arms and smothering him in kisses.

"Hey, whoa there! Stop that! You'll ruin my reputation!"

"Does Joan know?"

"No, I haven't told her yet."

"Well, we must tell her – now!"

Paula rushed inside, a new spring in her step, just as Tom passed her in the lobby heading out.

"Hello, stranger," Philippe smiled.

IN THE TIMELESS ancient land of Mother Africa, a new day dawned. A giant red glowing sun filled the horizon, silhouetting Charlene against a two-hundred-year-old tree. Free of his bandages, Shaka sat attentively by her side.

She raised a pair of binoculars to view a nursing leopard and her playful cubs.

"Look what we did, Shaka."

He barked.

Smiling at their beauty and relieved that for now at least they could live in dignity and freedom, she put down the binoculars and stroked Shaka, noticing Vernon's dog tags were still around his neck.

The morning sun rose eagerly in the sky, rapidly heating the surrounding plains. The dog tags would soon be too hot for the little Jack Russell to wear, so she slipped the collar off and ran her fingers over and over the well-worn numbers on the metal plating. She knew what he'd meant by leaving them – he really would have done anything for her. What a fool she'd been to shut him out.

Suddenly an elongated shadow smothered their position.

"I believe those belong to me," a voice said softly.

Shaka instantly jumped to his feet, dancing around Vernon, excitedly wagging his tail.

PLEASE VISIT THE WEBSITE HERE:
www.LandOfTheFreeMovie.com

You can donate to the cause here:
https://www.gofundme.com/a6u6s-land-of-the-free/donate

And within the United States here:
https://www.fracturedatlas.org/site/fiscal/profile?id=17808

Fractured Atlas is a 501(c)(3) public charity. Contributions for the purposes of Land of the Free are tax-deductible to the extent permitted by law.

AUTHOR’S FOOTNOTE

Meryl Harrison is one of the noblest, kindest and most courageous women on earth. She has given selflessly of her time, facing the very real threat of personal injury and death almost daily during her ten year tenure with the Zimbabwe NSPCA. She has ignored her own pain and well-being, while witnessing more horror than most could imagine and remain sane, to save the lives of precious and magnificent creatures that many of us don't spare a thought for.

During her tenure, Meryl’s twin brother was murdered by Mugabe supporters and her life partner died while she remained relentless in her quest to save and/or safeguard literally thousands of animals. Not surprisingly, this put an intolerable strain on her heart. In June, 2003, Meryl was in need of life-saving surgery she could not afford as 100% of her resources had been used in her welfare work.

Someone once said to me that no one should die because of a lack of money. That is true. But it is perhaps a little more true of Meryl.

By way of example, a week before Meryl was told she needed surgery, she arrived to negotiate with "war veterans" - so young that they could not have fought in Zimbabwe's liberation war – for the safe release of animals kept in the most shocking of conditions.

The “vets” told her to leave immediately. One of the youngsters came at her with an axe and insisted that she dance and sing Pamberina ZANU-PF with them (one of the anthems of Mr Mugabe's party). She had previously always successfully refused such demands, but on this occasion she surrendered. "The axe-man was too threatening and insistent. I didn't want to be a dead heroine, so I did it," she said.

Meryl has survived time and again because she has a sense of the ridiculous. It was just another day in her work, which has put such strain on her heart.

Listeners to the John Robbie Show on Talk Radio 702 in South Africa heard of her plight and pledged almost 60,000 South African Rand and offered material assistance for her operation. A heart surgeon even pledged surgery services for free.

"It was an extraordinary outpouring of charity," Robbie said. "We spoke to her on Tuesday; her story was amazing. Afterwards, on air, I asked her how much she would need for the operation, and she said R60 000. We didn't launch a special appeal but just mentioned that perhaps listeners may be able to help."

The station was inundated with calls of support in cash and kind: "We had pledges, offers of flights from three different airport companies, and ambulance services, among others."

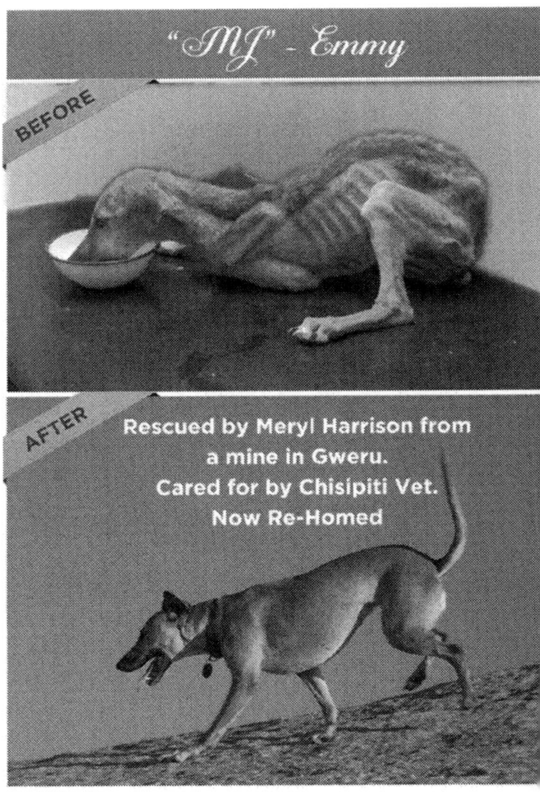

One Friday, Harrison, who had another busy week rescuing animals, said she was overwhelmed at the generosity of the people who had offered her financial and material help. "I was on my way to the farm when I received a call. I just parked on the side of the road and began to cry."

A history of Lynn's work with animal welfare

Lynn's first award for raising funds for animal welfare was received when she was just 11 years old, from the PDSA (People's Dispensary for Sick Animals, UK). She still proudly hangs on her wall the certificate she received for "Outstanding Effort".

In 1997 Lynn worked with Virginia McKenna OBE (who played Joy Adamson in the immortal classic "Born Free" and subsequently founded The Born Free Foundation in the UK) to rescue a lioness called Kimba from Italy. Kimba was discovered in a cage no bigger than she was, unable to see the sky, fed on a diet of frozen chickens. Her back was concave, her condition squalid. When Lynn saw Kimba freed and exploring her new home in the Big Cat Sanctuary of Kent, England, marveling at clouds rolling by, she wept, knowing she had found her true purpose in life.

In working with the Born Free Foundation, Lynn came to know Sir Roger Gale, MP (UK) who was then Chairman of the Parliamentary Committee on Animal Welfare. He subsequently became Vice Chairman of the Conservative Party, Chairman of the Conservation Group on Animal Welfare and spearheaded the ban of fox hunting in Britain. Roger has become a lifelong friend and remains in close liaison with Lynn on many animal welfare issues.

In 1998 Lynn was honored by WSPA (World Society for Protection of Animals). In recognition of funds she raised for that cause, Lynn was invited to inspect the WSPA sanctuary for rescued big brown bears in outback Turkey (formerly "Dancing Bears"). This sanctuary was in a very remote area of Turkey, near the Syrian border and absolutely not open to the public.

In 1999, Lynn was made the first and only honorary Life Member of the AfriCat UK Project 2000. Lynn has been in Africa many times, and been hands-on with the big cats that

AfriCat rescue, rehabilitate, and relocate. In 1999, when her first novel was released, Lynn donated the royalties to the AfriCat Foundation. Lise Hanssen, who then ran AfriCat in Namibia, joined Lynn is London's most famous department store, Harrods, for a joint book signing of this best-seller.

While Lynn was living in London she coincidentally became the neighbor of The (late) Hon Juanita Carberry of "White Mischief" fame (daughter of the late Lord Carberry). Juanita was a close personal friend of George and Joy Adamson. She was born and raised in Kenya. At the age of 78, Juanita resigned her position on the International Advisory Board of WSPA, and she bequeathed her drawings of Elsa by Joy Adamson to Lynn in her Will. The original paintings are in the National Museum of Nairobi.

In 2002 and 2003, Lynn was invited to be a judge by the RSPCA at their Million Paws Walk on the Gold Coast of Australia.

Lynn has also donated a major original oil on canvas to WWF (the World Wildlife Fund) which was auctioned at a special event organized in conjunction with Dreamworld's "Tiger Island" in 2003.

Lynn retains an extremely close relationship with Meryl Harrison, formerly the Chief Inspector of the Zimbabwe National Society for the Prevention of Cruelty to Animals. In 2001 Lynn brought Meryl out to Australia to meet with Tippi Hedren to discuss an exposé on unethical hunting.

See more of Lynn Santer at:

www.LynnSanter.com

PLEASE VISIT THE WEBSITE HERE:
www.LandOfTheFreeMovie.com

You can donate to the cause here:
https://www.gofundme.com/a6u6s-land-of-the-free/donate

And within the United States here:
https://www.fracturedatlas.org/site/fiscal/profile?id=17808

Fractured Atlas is a 501(c)(3) public charity. Contributions for the purposes of Land of the Free are tax-deductible to the extent permitted by law.

UNLIKELY HEROES

An unlikely team of 'heroes' was formed by necessity, in the face of unimaginable adversity, to tackle a job that no one else seemed willing to take on...
from Style Living – Gold Coast edition June-July 2003.

When Gold Coast award-winning author Lynn Santer, Hollywood movie legend Tippi Hedren, ex-NCA operative Reg Dickason, ex-SAS commando Dave Woodman, and an International RSPCA Bravery Award winner, Meryl Harrison, joined forces to help stop the killing of endangered big game in Zimbabwe, by some of the richest men on Earth, something unbelievable happened.

When iconic movie star Tippi Hedren, Alfred Hitchcock's star of *The Birds* and *Marnie*, was first contacted by Gold Coast author Lynn Santer, she may well have thought she had slipped into the fantasy world of one of Tinsel Town's creative minds. But the story that unfolded was all too real.

Lynn and Tippi had formed a strong friendship some years earlier through their mutual interest and tireless work in conserving the big cats of Africa. As one of the names listed to contact for help, on international animal welfare supporters lists, Lynn had received a cry for help from two-time international bravery award winner, Meryl Harrison (chief inspector with the Zimbabwe National SPCA).

Meryl told Lynn that the giant hunting group, Safari Club International - SCI (who includes among its membership such luminaries as George Bush Snr, General "Stormin' Norman" Schwartzkopf, and Dan Quayle), had managed to get 'special permits' to hunt endangered big game by some of the most brutal methods imaginable - methods even objected to by other hunters, as well as the CEO of the Hunting Association of Zimbabwe.

These methods had been outlawed in Zimbabwe. Yet for the might of the American dollar these illegal and barbaric methods were permitted for SCI members. Despite the fact that it is reported that a staggering eighty percent of Zimbabwe's wildlife has now been lost to hunting and poaching; despite Harrison risking her own life on a daily basis in an attempt to expose this situation; because of the $US70 million per year the industry brings into Zimbabwe, and because of the political weight of some of the hunters; no network seemed willing to take the risk of obtaining the evidence required to expose these atrocities.

Lynn felt she might have well been living on Mars - what could she do from the Gold Coast in Australia? But a phone call to Tippi Hedren later, the two began planning to bring these three ladies together on the same continent at the same time; to plan a covert operation with ex SAS commandos, who would go undercover as hunters in order to obtain footage and documented evidence of these atrocities.

Despite the need for relative anonymity in their work, both security expert, Reg Dickason and his partner Dave Woodman (a former Major, with ten years experience in the elite Special Air Service), were present at the special media book launch staged recently, enthusiastically lending their names and indeed faces to the event. “We wanted to corroborate what was in the book. The fact is, all this really happened,” said Dickason. Meryl was able to smuggle out information from the Zimbabwe Department of National Parks and Wildlife, which contained names of hunters, dates, locations, types of animals to be hunted, methods of hunting and the country of origin of the hunters, to assist this unlikely group of collaborators to coordinate their mission.

The methods of hunting included leopard hunts with packs of hounds that were “trained” with electric shock collars; the use of live bait (such as donkeys and goats) often left tied to a tree, where they were nibbled alive by scavengers for days before the predator came to take the bait; the use of hand guns and bows with barbed arrows (and no proficiency tests were required for the hunters), and the blatant statement - that fees would be charged for the hunts “whether the trophy is taken or whether the animal is wounded and lost”.

Some footage was obtained (which Lynn has safely locked away) showing in sickening detail, dogs being used to hunt big cats and a ‘canned hunt’ whereby big cats are left in tiny cages and ‘hunters’ literally shoot them at point blank through the cage bars. However it seemed this was still not enough to entice the networks to run with the story.

"So, we just decided some months after that, the best way to get the story out would be through the book," said Lynn.

Currently Lynn is working with a co-writer reworking her book for a film script. With interest already starting to grow from movie producers, we may soon see this amazing story on the big screen.

"But for now, to help stop the killing we have to raise awareness - and that starts with this book," said Lynn. As
an indication of Lynn's significant position on the world scene, when an important member of the British Government, Chris Daykin, the man credited in the UK as being Prime Minister Blair's right hand advisor on all matters financial, slipped quietly into Australia on official business recently, he made a radical departure from his global advisory role.

The dark-suited sage in London's House of Commons, squeezed time between official engagements in Sydney and on the Sunshine Coast, to visit with his old friend, on the Gold Coast - Lynn Santer.

"Chris was a great help to me when I penned the sequel to my first best seller 'Sins of Life'", said Lynn. Lynn and Chris had become friends when she was working in London as a specialist advisor on pensions reform legislation. "I couldn't be happier that such an important man shares the passion that I have for the big cats," said Lynn.

"Lynn has a passion for life, and a free and frank manner that is thoroughly refreshing," Chris said with a broad smile while enjoying canapés and cocktails in Lynn's Gold Coast home.

"Lynn is sadly missed in London," said Chris. "But now I have tasted a sample of life on the Gold Coast, I understand why she is reluctant to return."

See more of Lynn Santer at:

www.LynnSanter.com

Lynn, Tippi and Meryl
Jupiters Casino
2001

Lynn and Tippi
Launching the first edition of
LAND OF THE FREE
at The Grove, Los Angeles
2004

Lynn and Tippi 2017

Lynn introduces Tippi to her new Hollywood production partner, James Ganiere, CEO of RioVista Universal 2015

Lynn and James at the 2015 Emmys
(just after Cecil the lion was slaughtered)

Lynn at the AfriCat Foundation
Namibia, 1999

Lynn with Dave Woodman and
Reg Dickason at the Australian launch of
LAND OF THE FREE 2003

Meryl Harrison

To the fallen by Lynn Santer

Spare a thought today for those who run in fear,
and for those around the world who helpless shed a tear.
Endangered wildlife is being tortured by those who do believe,
it is their right to slaughter – it should cause your soul to freeze.

This is not myth or fiction, in fact dateline now, today,
this is what is unfolding for the blood money they pay.
A donkey's left alive and tied, baying for its life,
and so a leopard stealthily approaches to its strife.

A pack of dogs are then released to chase the hapless cat,
electric collars round their throats to show them where it's at.
If any dog defies their man a shock is soon released,
the dog spins and then it vomits in silent disbelief.

Thinking this is sport, men approach the cat that is their prize,
with lustful greed and ego they see a trophy before their eyes.
The leopard has a cub back home, the hope of future years,
in running for her life the cub senses mum's deep fears.

A bullet strikes into her leg, the leopard cries in pain,
but the men who hunt her only care for what they have to gain.
Her head spins with pain and anguish, she runs with all her might,
but with hounds snapping at her heels it's really not much of a
fight.

The men close in, they do not care she could be the last feline
to rule the land that God gave her to live in quite sublime.
They care only for proving "manhood", for trophies on the wall,
leaving orphans, pain and suffering, to them this is a ball.

This is not myth or fiction, it is happening now, today,
if your voices still stay silent, things will go on this way,
until one day, and very soon, the last of her kind will say,
"It's too late now to save me, extinction comes my way."

So stop what it is you're doing, put down the milk and bread,
stand in a minute's silence and think of what I've said.
To say "it's sad" and go about your business of the day,
justifies the men who demand to hunt big game this way.

The message you are sending is that it really is okay,
so long as thirty silver coins in advance you have had to pay.
Is that what you want to tell the world, that you'll stand and let them be?
Or do you want to take a stand for them to live as born, born free?

PLEASE VISIT THE WEBSITE HERE:
www.LandOfTheFreeMovie.com

You can donate to the cause here:
https://www.gofundme.com/a6u6s-land-of-the-free/donate

And within the United States here:
https://www.fracturedatlas.org/site/fiscal/profile?id=17808

Fractured Atlas is a 501(c)(3) public charity. Contributions for the purposes of Land of the Free are tax-deductible to the extent permitted by law.

EXTINCTION IS FOREVER

Printed in Great Britain
by Amazon

78226114R00077